LATIMER STUDIES 71

EMPTY AND EVIL

THE WORSHIP OF OTHER FAITHS IN 1 CORINTHIANS 8–10 AND TODAY

BY ROHINTAN KEKI MODY

The Latimer Trust

Empty and Evil: The worship of other faiths in 1 Corinthians 8-10 and today © Rohintan Keki Mody 2009

ISBN 978-0-946307-72-2

Cover photo © OlegD – Fotolia.com

Published by the Latimer Trust January 2010

The Latimer Trust (formerly Latimer House, Oxford) is a conservative Evangelical research organisation within the Church of England, whose main aim is to promote the history and theology of Anglicanism as understood by those in the Reformed tradition. Interested readers are welcome to consult its website for further details of its many activities.

The Latimer Trust
PO Box 26685, London N14 4XQ UK
Registered Charity: 1084337
Company Number: 4104465
Web: www.latimertrust.org
E-mail: administrator@latimertrust.org

CONTENTS

Introduction

> The principal crime of the human race, the highest guilt charged upon the world, the whole procuring cause of judgement, is idolatry.
>
> Tertullian, *On Idolatry*, 1

> All inhabitants of the earth will worship the beast – all whose names have not been written in the book of life belonging to the Lamb that was slain from the creation of the world.
>
> Revelation 13:8

We live in multi-faith nations. Hindu, Muslim, Sikh, and Buddhist communities populate our cities. The presence of other faiths raises complex theological and practical issues.

When I was a curate in Wolverhampton, the clergy was invited to a deanery chapter meeting at the local offices of the Wolverhampton inter–faith society. Wolverhampton is a multi-faith city, containing Hindu, Sikh, and Buddhist temples (and the city has a mosque). At that meeting (at which were only local Anglican clergy) we were led through the prayers and Scripture readings of Hinduism, Sikhism, Buddhism, Islam, and Judaism. The organizers came from an evangelical background but justified their actions because they were building links with the other faith communities. They believed that Christ was the only saviour but faith in him on the part of those of other faiths in Wolverhampton was unnecessary for salvation, though desirable.

The subject raises large theological questions about the nature of other faiths and Christian participation in the worship of other faiths. Daily, across the world, millions of Christians face the issue of the consumption of food offered to other gods. A city like Mumbai is a city full of idols (cf. Acts 17:16). There are images of Hindu gods in shops, hotels taxis, and even lifts! Every Hindu home will have a household shrine with images of gods. Food offered to gods is central to religious ritual, weddings, birthday celebrations, and funerals. A great deal of family and social pressure is placed on Christians to participate in these social rituals and eat food offered to idols.

Yet, the issue of food offered to idols cannot be dismissed as of little real relevance in the West given the presence of large communities of those of other faiths in the UK. What if your Hindu neighbours invite you to their daughter's wedding in the temple? Do you go? What advice should a minister give to a Chinese convert who feels obliged to participate in ancestor worship? To go to the ceremony or not? If one goes, should one participate? If one does not go, how should one deal with fall-out from the family?

Thankfully, the Bible gives us answers to these questions since a great deal of the Bible was written in the context of a multi-faith society. In particular, Paul deals in depth with the issue of the relationship of the church to other faiths in 1 Corinthians 8–10.

The religious environment of Corinth in the first century was pluralistic. Some Corinthian Christians argue in their letter to Paul that they have a right to eat food offered to idols (1 Corinthians 8:1,9). For them, there is no reality to the pagan "gods" represented by the idols as there is only one God (1 Corinthians 8:4). Paul agrees but qualifies his agreement by insisting that not only is God one but that his uniqueness must finally determine the way Christians relate to other faiths (8:4–6).[1]

In chapter 10:18–22 Paul affirms that not only is pagan worship idolatrous but that demons are somehow related to the worship of pagan gods and idols. For a Christian to participate in the worship of other faiths is to risk involvement in the world of evil powers.

---

[1] G.D. Fee, *The First Epistle to the Corinthians* (Grand Rapids: Eerdmans, 1987), 376.

All too frequently, Western exegesis has focused on reading 1 Corinthians 8–10 through the lens of Romans 14–15 as delineating the nature of Christian liberty; that food is always a morally neutral matter (an *adiaphoron*). Thus, it has missed Paul's distinctive and complex treatment of idolatry and evil powers.

In 1 Corinthians 8:4–5 and 10:18–22 Paul seems to affirm that pagan gods are powerless idols and yet are also evil and powerful. This apparent paradox raises the question of how the worship of pagan gods can be a worship that is both vain and yet real. This study seeks to examine Paul's thought about *the nature of the relationship between powers of evil and idols in 1 Corinthians 10:18–22 and its theological and pastoral implications for today.*

This passage is the climax of Paul's discussion in chapters 8–10, while chapters 8–10 are themselves the longest and most detailed discussion that Paul undertakes on idolatry. These reasons make it the most important passage in the Pauline corpus on the relationship between evil powers and idols. This study will first examine Paul's understanding of idols/idolatry and demons (chapter 1). Chapter 2 will look at the relationship between demons and idols, and, finally, chapter 3 will focus on the theological and pastoral implications for ministry today.

1. Idols and Demons in 1 Corinthians 8–10

> What profit is the idol when its maker has carved it, an image; a teacher of falsehood? For its maker trusts in his handiwork – fashioning speechless idols.
>
> Habakkuk 2:18

> And there was a man in the synagogue possessed by the spirit of an unclean demon, and he cried out with a loud voice, "Ha! What do we have to do with you, Jesus of Nazareth? Have you come to destroy us? I know who you are – the Holy One of God!"
>
> Luke 4:33–34

In 1 Corinthians 10:19f. Paul links demons with idols: "What do I mean? That food offered to idols is anything or that an idol is anything? No, but what they sacrifice they sacrifice to demons and to what is not God."[2] Paul's statement raises important questions: What is an idol? What is idolatry? Who are the demons? This chapter will focus on the questions of the nature of idols and idolatry, and the identity of the demons within the context of 1 Corinthians 8–10.

---

[2] Other passages that may relate evil powers and worship according to some scholars include 2 Corinthians 6:14-7:1; Ephesians 6:12; and 1 Corinthians 15:24. For 2 Corinthians 6:14-7:1 see the discussions in W.J. Webb, *Returning Home: New Covenant and Second Exodus as the Context for 2 Corinthians 6.14-7.1* (Sheffield: JSOT, 1993), 200-215. For Ephesians 6:12 see the discussion in H.W. Hoehner, *Ephesians: An Exegetical Commentary* (Grand Rapids: Baker, 2002), 827.

1.1. The Context of 1 Corinthians 8–10

Before we can consider the nature of idols/idolatry and the identity of the demons, we need to understand the context of 1 Corinthians 8–10. In 1 Corinthians 8–10 Paul responds to the questions posed in the Corinthian church's letter to him about the complex subject of food offered to idols (8:1; cf. 7:1). The subject of food offered to idols is complex because food offered to idols could be eaten in the idol temple (8:10), as part of sacrifices to idols (10:20f.), be bought from the market place (10:25), and eaten at dinners in people's homes (10:27f.).

In addition, we need understand why some Corinthian Christians were eating food offered to idols. They could justify the practice theologically because they have "knowledge" that there is only One God and idols do not exist (8:1, 4). For them, since pagan gods do not exist, participation in idol feasts are merely matters of good food, good company, and good fun. What did it matter to participate in feasts in the temple of Zeus, if Zeus did not exist?

Socially, the Corinthians Christians lived in a multi-faith society; there were Greek, Roman, and Egyptian cults in Corinth. They had the civic and social "right" to attend idol feasts (8:9). They were under social and cultural pressure to attend their families' and friends' weddings, funerals, birthday celebrations etc. in the local idol temples. In other words, Corinth was similar to some of our multi-faith cities today.

Paul responds to these issues by making a number of distinct points. In 8:1–3 he asserts that that the Corinthian Christians' "knowledge" must be shaped and qualified by love for God. In 8:4–6, he agrees with the Corinthians' catchphrases that there is only one God and idols not exist. However, Paul insists that Christians cannot ignore the social phenomenon of pagan beliefs in many gods in deciding whether to participate in idol feasts (8:5a). In addition, he asserts that Christian worship is exclusive because there is one God, the Father, and one Lord, Jesus Christ, and this uniqueness precludes participation in idol feasts (8:6).

In 8:7–13 Paul argues that "rights" need to be set aside for the sake of new Christians who lack an understanding of monotheism and who may be led back into idolatry by the behaviour of the "knowers." In chapter 9, Paul illustrates the setting aside of rights by pointing to his own example of voluntary renunciation of his "rights" for the sake of the gospel.

In 10:1–13 Paul brings up the Scriptural case of Israel at the time of the exodus and in the wilderness as a typological model for the church. As Israel was redeemed from slavery in Egypt, so the church has been redeemed from slavery to sin (10:1–4 cf. 5:7f.). Israel rebelled by falling into idolatry in the wilderness but the church must not repeat Israel's mistakes in the wilderness of pagan Corinth (10:6–13). In 10:14–17 Paul argues the Corinthians must avoid idol feasts by talking about the spiritual benefits of the Lord's Supper as the holy counterpart of idol feasts.

In 10:18–22 he warns that idolatry is ultimately demonic and Christians who enjoy the Lord's Table cannot partake in the table of demons. The table of demons is a counterfeit of the Lord's Table. In 10:23–11:1 Paul deals with the remaining issues arising from his rejection of Corinthian participation in idol feasts; that of whether it is permissible to eat food from the market (which may have originated in the idol temple); whether to accept the dinner invitations of pagans; and whether to eat food at a dinner which may have come from the idol temple.

To sum up, Paul writes chapters 8–10 as a reply to the concerns expressed in the Corinthians' letter about food offered to idols. Paul is attempting to dissuade the Corinthians from attending idol feasts. He points out that the worship of the One God is exclusive and that demons are associated with idols. Having looked at the context, we can now examine Paul's definition of idols/idolatry in 1 Corinthians 8 and 10.

1.2. *The nature of idols and idolatry in 1 Corinthians 8 and 10.*

In 1 Corinthians 8–10, Paul uses the term "idol" (*eidōlon*) in 8:4;

8:7; 10:19. However, what does Paul mean by "idol" and "idolatry"? In this section, I shall consider what Paul means by "idol" in 1 Corinthians 8:4, and then consider the idolatry of Israel in 10:18–20.

1.2.1.   *1 Corinthians 8:4*

In 1 Corinthians 8:1–3 Paul responds to the questions that the Corinthian Christians wrote to him, regarding the subject of food offered to idols. Paul quotes one of their "catchphrases" that "all of us possess 'knowledge'" (v. 1a). But, Paul immediately qualifies this "catchphrase" by pointing out that "knowledge" puffs up, but love builds up (v. 1b). Paul continues by asserting that if anyone thinks they have mastered this "knowledge" they do not truly "know" (v. 2). Rather, anyone who loves God is known by him (v. 3).

In v. 4, Paul then explains the content of the "knowledge":

> Therefore, regarding the eating of food offered to idols (*eidōlothutōn*), we know that "no idol (*eidōlon*) has any reality in the universe" because "there is no God but one."

The "knowledge" in this verse is knowledge about the unreality of *eidōla*. It is likely that Paul does use *eidōlon* here to signify both the non–existence of the pagan gods and the vanity of cult images.

Eidōlon in 1 Corinthians 8:4 is used in the sense of a non–existent pagan god itself and a spiritually lifeless cult image, and represents Paul's agreement with the Corinthians.[3] *Eidōlon* has associations of something that is a copy and appears to have substance, but in reality, is insubstantial, and, hence, can be deceptive.

Therefore, in 8:4, pagans believe the *eidōlon* to be a real living god, but Christians know the truth, the god itself is a fiction. The god is merely imaginary and its cult image has no spiritual

---

[3] So J. Calvin, *1 Corinthians: Calvin's New Testament Commentaries* (Grand Rapids/Carlisle: Eerdmans/Paternoster, 1996), 173.

reality. Indeed the phrase verges on the tautologous: "no non-existent thing exists in the world."[4] Here then, an idol is both the spiritually unreal cult image and the non-existent pagan god.[5] So, for Paul, Zeus does not exist. Zeus is a counterfeit god. The cult image of Zeus has no spiritual reality.

The second "catchphrase," is a confession "there is no God but One," and alludes to the *Shema* of Deuteronomy 6:4. The "catchphrase" asserts that the God of the Bible is real and is the *only* Deity who exists, which implies that all gods as conceived by pagans are false and unreal.[6]

1 Corinthians 8:4 is important in the context of chapters 8–10 because it reveals Paul's view of the nature of the pagan gods and cult images of the gods: they are both "idols." Paul uses *eidōlon* (idol) here in the sense both of the non-existence of the pagan gods and the spiritual unreality of cult images of the pagan gods. In this case, the phrase means, "a pagan god has no existence in the universe and its cult image has no spiritual life."

Therefore, Paul rejects the pagan notions of the existence of pagan gods and the spiritual reality of cult images. Paul's beliefs are based on the unique and exclusive identity of the One true God as revealed in Christ.[7] Thus, Paul defines an idol to be the non-existent pagan god itself and its cult image. Gordon Fee puts it well when he says of the "catchphrases" in 1 Corinthians 8:4:

---

[4] D. Newton, *Deity and Diet: The Dilemma of Sacrificial Food at Corinth* (Sheffield: Sheffield Academic Press, 1998), 281.

[5] In 8:4, Paul cannot be referring to the *physical unreality* of the cult image since clearly the cult image does have *physical reality*, see Newton, *Deity*, 286.

[6] Newton, *Deity*, 286.

[7] Deuteronomy 4:35; 39; 6:4f.; Isaiah 45:5, 14, 21f.; 46:9; Joel 2:27; Zechariah 14:9; Malachi 2:10; Matthew 22:37; Mark 12:29-32; Luke 10:27; 1 Timothy 2:5; James 2:19, cf. Romans 3:28ff.; Galatians 3:20; Ephesians 4:4ff.

An idol lacks any reality. Although there is some ambiguity as to its precise nuance, what they almost certainly mean is that there is no reality to Isis or Sarapis or Asclepius. Idols yes; but genuine reality, no. This is because of the basic statement of the Christian faith, "There is no God but one."[8]

1.2.2. *Idolatry in 1 Corinthians 10:18–19*

Paul's view of idolatry is related to his view of an idol. In 1 Corinthians 10:1–13 Paul alludes to the story of Israel in the wilderness and warns the church not to repeat Israel's mistakes. In 10:14–17 Paul describes the spiritual implications of the Lord's Supper. In v. 18, Paul continues to talk about the spiritual implications of religious meals and asks the Corinthians to "consider Israel according to the flesh; are not those who eat the sacrifices common participants in the altar?" In this phrase, Paul probably stresses the sins of Israel in the OT, since Paul has already talked about the sins of Israel in 10:6–11.

In 10:7, Paul warns the Corinthians not to commit idolatry as some of the Israelites did and then quotes Exodus 32:6 (the golden calf incident). In v. 18, Paul may invite his readers to cast their minds back to Paul's account of the wilderness rebellion in vv. 6–11.[9] The quotation itself focuses not upon the making of the golden calf, but upon the *eating* (*phagein*), drinking, and dancing that follow the making of the golden calf. It suggests that Paul's focus in v. 7 is to underline the importance of staying away from pagan feasts. Importantly, the point here is that any participation in an act of homage or reverence or honour to an idol constitutes idolatry.

---

[8] Fee, *The First Epistle* to *the Corinthians*, 371.

[9] R.D. Hays, *Echoes of Scripture in the Letters of Paul* (New Haven/London: Yale University Press, 1989), 93.

Paul's thought in 1 Corinthians 10:18f. is as follows: the Israelites, by sharing the food on a pagan altar, are partners in idolatrous worship (v. 18). The possible inference by a reader that this implies that both food offered to idols and the idol itself have spiritual reality (v. 19) is a false inference: "What then do I mean to affirm and imply? That food sacrificed to idols has any spiritual reality, or that an idol has any spiritual reality?" Paul's purpose here is to argue that Israel's idolatry establishes a common partnership (*koinōnia*) in pagan worship.

If Paul is asking his Corinthian readers to cast their minds back to Israel's idolatrous eating in the wilderness, then Paul asks Christians today to do the same. Christians must never forget that their forefathers committed idolatry when then built and worshipped the golden calf, and that if the ancient people of God committed idolatry throughout their history then Christians are not immune from the same temptation (1 Corinthians 10:13f.). Christians must take heed of the sad story of OT Israel (1 Corinthians 10:6–11), and not repeat their mistake.

Paul, in 1 Corinthians 8–10, defines an "idol" as a spiritually lifeless cult image/physical representation in stone, wood, or metal of a pagan deity, and *also* a pagan god itself, thought to really exist by pagans but dismissed by Paul as false, unreal, and imaginary.[10] The pagan gods and their cult images are counterfeits. An idol is, as Paul says, in v. 20, "what is not God (*kai ou theō*)."[11] Paul defines "idolatry" as being any ritual or cultic act that involves the invocation of, payment of homage or honour, or worship of, an idol. Having considered the subject of idols and idolatry, we can now turn to the issue of the identity of the demons.

---

[10] Note however, Paul's equation of greed with idolatry in Ephesians 5:5; Colossians 3:5. See B.S. Rosner, *Greed as Idolatry* (Grand Rapids: Eerdmans, 2007) for a full discussion of the idolatrous aspects of greed.

[11] P.D. Gardner, *The Gifts of God and the Authentication of a Christian: An Exegetical Study of 1 Corinthians 8-11:1* (Lanham: University Press of America, 1994), 167.

1.3. The identity of the Demons (1 Corinthians 10:20f.)

In 1 Corinthians 10:19 Paul denies that idols and idolatry have any spiritual reality. Yet in v. 20a, Paul insists that idolatry is not merely empty, but it is also dark and evil: "No, rather I imply that what they [the Israelites] sacrifice, 'they sacrifice to demons, and to what is not God,' and I really do not want you to become partners (*koinōnous*) in demons." Paul asserts (alluding to Deuteronomy 32:17) that participation by Christians in pagan meals involves sacrifices to *daimonia* (demons). It means that Christians are somehow involved with demons.[12]

Not only is paganism idolatrous it is also associated with the demonic. *Therefore, in v. 20, Paul, with one pregnant phrase, affirms that pagan sacrifices are both to demons and to cult images.* However, who are demons in 1 Corinthians 10:20f.? Can the demons be classified within the taxonomy for evil powers? This section will examine the issue of the personal identity of the *daimonia*.[13] There are three possibilities that I will consider.

1.3.1. The Principalities and Powers

First, the demons may be included with the rubric of the principalities and powers of evil.

There are key reference to supernatural principalities and powers in Ephesians. In 1:21 Christ is seated in the heavenlies "far

---

[12] The word *daimonion* can have a substantial semantic range, see H.G. Liddell, R. Scott, H.J. Jones, *A Greek-English Lexicon with a Revised Supplement* (Oxford: Clarendon, 1996), 365.

[13] By "personal being," I mean "particular sentient living beings with the capacity for thought, purposeful activity, and verbal communication, and relationships." Note also 1 Timothy 4:1: "The Holy Spirit expressly says that in later times some will depart from the faith by devoting themselves to deceitful spirits and the teachings of demons," and James 2:19, "even the demons believe – and shudder." In these passages, the demons are clearly personal supernatural beings since they deceive, teach, believe, and shudder in anticipation of God's judgement on their evil activities.

above all rule (*archēs*) and authority (*exousias*) and power (*dunameōs*) and lordship (*kuriotēs*), and above every name (*onomatos*) that is named." Christ's power is above all other spiritual powers.

Yet in 2:2, the Ephesians, before they came to Christ, used to follow "the ruler (*archonta*) of the kingdom of the air, the spirit who is now at work in those who are disobedient." Here spiritual powers can adversely and powerfully influence humanity. In 3:10 the existence of the church shows that God's wisdom is "made known to the rulers (*archais*) and authorities (*exousias*) in the heavenly realms." The church's existence is a witness to God's wisdom and power over all other spiritual powers.

In 6:12 Christians:

> do not wrestle against flesh and blood, but against the rulers (*archas*), the authorities (*exousias*) and the cosmic powers (*kosmokratoras*) over this present darkness, against the spiritual forces (*pneumatika*) of evil (*ponerias*) in the heavenly places.

Christians are involved in spiritual warfare, not against earthly powers, but against heavenly powers. Clearly, in these texts in Ephesians, the locus of these powers in the "heavenly realms" means that they must be supernatural and their opposition to the purposes of God and Christ means that they are evil. Yet the terminology of "rule," "authorities,", and "powers" is abstract and collective and implies that they are powerful structural and corporate entities of evil.

How then are these corporate structures of evil connected with demons, personal beings? The principalities and powers may be "made up" of demons. The terminology of "demons" implies that these evil powers are individual and personal beings, while the terminology of "principalities" and "powers" may stress that evil powers are also structural corporate entities.[14]

These supernatural principalities and powers "made up" of demons may then influence human social and political structures and organizations which inflict suffering and evil. Neil Elliott rightly notes that, in Paul, "the work of 'heavenly' Powers opposed to God ('angels, principalities') is clearly described as being carried out through very human instruments: 'oppression, distress, persecution, starvation, destitution, peril, sword' (Romans 8:35–39)."[15]

For us today, it means that demons are active through political, social, and religious structures. Thus, it is possible that demons may exert an influence on Islamic fundamentalist governments and societies, so that they perpetrate unjust religious and social policies. The same may apply to the UK; as the culture of our society becomes increasingly post-Christian, our society may increasingly be influenced in its structures by demons in areas such as sexual morality, abortion, euthanasia etc.

A contemporary analogy may help to clarify. Thus, to say that, "the government today announced its strategy for the war in Afghanistan" puts the stress upon the governing political structure and its power (which is impersonal). Yet the government is "made up" of individual civil servants and their ministers (who are persons). The two are distinct though overlapping categories. The same may be true of the relationship between principalities/powers and demons. The principalities and powers (impersonal structures) may be "made up" of *daimonia* (personal beings) and the demons may operate through the supernatural structures of principalities and powers. The terminology of principalities and powers may

---

[14] See the discussion of principalities and powers in O'Brien, "Principalities and Powers: Opponents of the Church" in *Biblical Interpretation and the Church: Text and Context* (ed. D.A. Carson; Exeter: Paternoster, 1984), 110-154.
[15] N. Elliott, "The Anti-Imperial Message of the Cross" in *Paul and Empire: Religion and Power in Roman Imperial Society* (ed. R.A. Horsley; Harrisburg: Trinity, 1997), 179.

stress the structural dimensions of evil, while the terminology of *daimonia*/demons may stress the personal identity of evil powers.[16]

1.3.2. *The Angels of the Nations*

The second possible identification, that the demons are the angels of the nations, is related to the concept of the powers and principalities. Here Deuteronomy 32 and Daniel 10 are important. In the Song of Moses, in LXX Deuteronomy 32:8, Moses says that supernatural beings have authority over the nations and, implicitly, over the pagan religions of the nations:

> When the Most High was apportioning the nations, as he scattered the sons of Adam, he fixed the boundaries of the nations according to the number of the sons of God.[17]

Here the sons of God are supernatural beings "in charge" of the nations. The phrase "sons of God" in Deuteronomy 32:8 clearly refers to supernatural beings since most of the textual witnesses to the LXX read "angels of God" (*angelōn theou*) which makes the supernatural identity of these beings explicit, while in Deuteronomy 32:43 the "sons of God" are placed in parallel to the

---

[16] Forbes argues distinctly that Paul saw evil powers as a combination of personal spirits (demons) and abstractions (powers and principalities) and that Paul cannot be understood as having demythologized apocalyptic demonology. C. Forbes, "Paul's Principalities and Powers: Demythologizing Apocalyptic?" *JSNT* 82 (2001), 61. See also the discussions of principalities and powers in the Pauline corpus in W. Wink, *Naming the Powers. The Language of Power in the New Testament* (vol. 1 of *The Powers*; Philadelphia: Fortress, 1984), 13-21; 99-148; P.T. O'Brien, "Principalities and Powers: Opponents of the Church," in *Biblical Interpretation and the Church. Text and Context* (ed. D.A. Carson; Exeter: Paternoster, 1984), 110-150; and my, *The Relationship Between Powers of Evil and Idols in 1 Corinthians 8:4-5 and 10:18-22 in the Context of the Pauline Corpus and Early Judaism* (Ph.D Thesis, University of Aberdeen, 2008), 289-296.

[17] In this study, "OG" means the Old Greek text of the Old Testament and the Septuagint (LXX) means the translation of the Pentateuch alone rather than the original Greek translations of the OT. All quotations of German and French works are given in my own translations.

"angels of God."[18] This view of supernatural powers existing in the heavenly places is consistent with the concept of the heavenly court in the OT. In Job 1–2, Satan is present in the heavenly court. In 1 Kings 22:19b–22; Zechariah 3:1–7, the "sons of God" (angelic courtiers) are arrayed around God's throne.[19] In Psalm 82:1, 6, God judges the "sons of the Most High," rulers over the nations, in the heavenly court for their rebellion. [20]

There is further support for this option and the concept of the angels of the nations in Daniel 10. In Daniel 10:13–21 Michael, the angelic prince of Israel (cf. 12:1), is opposed by the angelic princes of Persia and Greece who rule these nations.[21] In Daniel 10:13, a great unnamed holy being fights the ruler of the Persians:

> And the ruler (*archōn*) of the kingdom of the Persians stood opposite me twenty–one days, and, behold, Michael, one of the chief rulers (*archontōn*), came to help me and I left him there with the ruler (*archontos*) of the Kingdom of the Persians.

This holy being then returns in v. 20 and speaks to Daniel:

> And he said, "do you know why I have come to you? And now I will return to fight against the ruler (*archontos*) of the Persians. And as I was leaving, the ruler (*archōn*) of the Greeks was coming."[22]

Here the rulers of the Persians and Greeks are probably supernatural beings since the ruler of the Persians is powerful enough to impede a holy angel in the execution of his commission

---

[18] See my, *Relationship,* 76-100.

[19] P.G. Bolt, "Defeat of the Evil Powers," in *Christ's Victory over Evil* (ed. P.G. Bolt; Nottingham: Apollos, 2009), 55.

[20] Psalm 82 is probably talking about evil angelic beings. See the discussion in my, *Relationship*, 82-85.

[21] See my *Relationship*, 85-87, for a full discussion.

[22] Translation is mine and is based on the textual witness of Theodotion to Greek Daniel.

for three weeks, "the ruler of the kingdom of the Persians stood opposite me twenty-one days." It is unlikely that these are the human rulers of the earthly kingdoms since it is unlikely that humans can impede the divine commission of holy beings. However, powerful supernatural beings in opposition to God's will would have the power to impede the mission of other (holy) supernatural beings.[23] The conflict here is on a supernatural level, "and now I will return to fight against the ruler of the Persians." Here it seems that that these figures are the patron angels of these nations. The protective role of Michael is in relation to the *people* of God rather than the physical *territory* and land of Israel.

Further, since the "the ruler of the kingdom of the *Persians/ the Greeks*," is a supernatural power, it is likely that these rulers have supernatural power over the socio-political structures of Persia and Greece rather than geographical boundaries (i.e. they are not "territorial spirits").[24] Thus, the issue is not territorial but political and personal. National angelic beings oppose God's carrying out of his purposes through his people Israel. There is spiritual warfare in the supernatural realm as the holy angels counter the malevolent influence of the supernatural ruler of the Persians upon the political situation on earth.[25] The earthly battles reflect the heavenly battles, whichever side wins in heaven wins on earth, "on earth as it is in heaven," (Matthew 6:10).[26] The supernatural rulers "stand behind" or, better, "above" the earthly rulers and kingdoms.

Later in Deuteronomy 32, in v. 17, (which Paul alludes to in 1 Corinthians 10:20) Moses records that Israel during its forty years in the wilderness sacrificed to demons: "they sacrificed to demons and to what is not God." The simplest option is to identify the

---

[23] D.E. Stevens, "Daniel 10 and the Notion of Territorial Spirits," *BSac* 157 (2000): 418.
[24] Stevens, "Daniel 10," 428-429.
[25] Stevens, "Daniel 10," 431.
[26] J.E. Goldingay, *Daniel*, (Nashville: Thomas Nelson, 1989), 291-292.

demons of Deuteronomy 32:17 with the sons of God/angelic rulers of the nations of v. 8. Paul clearly knows Deuteronomy 32 well given the allusion to Deuteronomy 32:17 in 1 Corinthians 10:20 and Deuteronomy 32:21 in 1 Corinthians 10:22 and Paul's other citations of Deuteronomy 32 (Romans 10:19, 12:19, 15:10).

Further, in 1 Corinthians 8:5b Paul asserts that behind the empty pagan cults there are evil powers: "there exist many 'gods' (*theoi*) and 'lords' (*kurioi*)." Jean Héring thinks that here Paul follows Jewish theology that there are a number of angelic beings, which men might be tempted to worship, and which are sometimes called "gods." He suggests that the "lords" in 1 Corinthians 8:5b may refer to the angels of the nations, hidden behind political powers (cf. the "lordship" of Ephesians 3:10).[27] Therefore, it is possible that Paul intends to identify the demons with the angels of the nations.

If the demons in 1 Corinthians 10:20f. are the angels of the nations there may be two ways in which the demons could exert their power over Corinth. First, there could be a demon in charge of a particular area and its cult within Corinth (i.e. a demon is a "territorial spirit"). However, Deuteronomy 32:8 and Daniel 10 suggest that one supernatural being has authority over an entire nation and its people rather than over territories and areas.

Since there are many different nationalities and cults in Corinth, it is possible that an individual demon has authority over the cults of one nationality or people group. Thus, today in, say, London, there would a demon in charge over, say Punjabi Hindu religion, one over Iranian Muslims, one over Thai Buddhists, etc. The demons may be under the authority of Satan, given the references to Satan in 1 Corinthians 5:5 and 7:5. The demons who rule over a nationality's cults may extend Satan's power and influence over the different nationalities and cults of Corinth and,

---

[27] J. Héring, *La Première Épître de Saint Paul aux Corinthiens* (Neuchâtel/Paris: Delachaux & Niestlé, 1949), 65.

indeed, in the world today.

1.3.3. The Spirits of the Dead Giants

The third possible identification is that the demons in 1 Corinthians 10:20f. may be the spirits of the dead giants of Genesis 6 infamy. This possible identification of the demons as the spirits of the dead giants might seem to be very odd for modern evangelicals but there is good evidence for this possibility.

In early Jewish traditions derived from the narrative of the sons of God marrying human women enshrined in Genesis 6:1–4 and Deuteronomy 32:8, 17, the sons of God or Watchers are angelic beings who rebel against God's creation order and marry human women.[28] The offspring of the Watchers and human women are the giants. These giants die during the flood. Because the nature of the giants is partly supernatural, spirits emanate from the dead bodies of the giants. These spirits of the dead giants are the demons and evil spirits behind pagan idols. Archie Wright, in his study, concludes that, "it is clear that the spirits of the giants assume an important place in the understanding of human suffering and the problem of evil within developing Second Temple period demonology and anthropology."[29]

The Old Greek version of the OT hints that the Watchers and giants traditions influenced the translators. The Old Greek translation of Genesis 6:4 uses the term "giant" (*gigas*) and records that "giants were on the earth in those days," and these giants were the offspring of the sons of God and human women. In addition,

---

[28] These Jewish traditions are especially found in *1 Enoch* chs 1-36 and *Jubilees.* See my *Relationship,* 121-153, for a full exegesis of these traditions.

[29] A.T. Wright, *The Origin of Evil Spirits* (Tübingen: Mohr Siebeck, 2005), 223. L.T. Stuckenbruck, "Giant Mythology and Demonology" in Demons: The Demonology of Israelite-Jewish and Early Christian Literature in Context of their Environment. (eds. A. Lange, H. Lichtenberger & K.F.D. Römheld; Tübingen: Mohr Siebeck, 2003), 318, fn. 2 notes the presence of the giants traditions in many early Jewish works.

in OG Isaiah 14:9, "giants" in Hades rise up to meet the descending shade of the King of Babylon. The Babylonian King, in v. 12, is called the "Day Star" fallen from heaven because of his hubris in attempting to be equal to God (v. 14; cf. Ezekiel 28). Thus, Isaiah 14 may perhaps allude to the developing traditions of the spirits of the dead giants. Further, Psalm 106 shows awareness that demons are connected with a cult of the dead. Psalm 106:28 records that Israel joined in the worship of Baal Peor and ate "sacrifices offered to the dead (*nekrōn*)" (cf. Numbers 25:1–3), while v. 37 states that Israel sacrificed "their sons and daughters to the demons." If we link vs. 28 and 37, then it implies that, in the Psalm, the demons are underworld powers.

In addition, in the NT, 1 Peter 3:19; 2 Peter 2:4 and Jude 6 probably show awareness of the Watchers traditions. 1 Peter 3:19f. says that Christ went and proclaimed his victory to the "spirits in prison who formerly did not obey, when God's patience waited in the days of Noah." The reference to the flood and "imprisoned spirits" means that Peter probably has the incarcerated Watchers in mind. 2 Peter 2:4 refers to God not sparing "the angels when they sinned, but cast them into Tartarus" at the time of the flood, which fits with the idea that these angels are probably the Watchers. Jude in v. 6 refers to, "angels who did not keep their own domain but abandoned their proper abode, He [God] has kept in eternal bonds under darkness for the judgment of the great day." This verse is a clear reference to the Watchers since Jude quotes from *1 Enoch* 1:9 in vv. 14–15.

Most importantly, there may be an echo of the Watchers traditions (the traditions about the angels/sons of God who fall in Genesis 6 by marrying human women) in 1 Corinthians 11:10.[30] In 1 Corinthians 11:2–16, following his discussion of food offered to idols in chapters 8–10, Paul considers the relationship between men and women in public worship, and the need for women to wear a head covering in public worship. In 11:10, Paul argues that,

---

[30] See my *Relationship*, 250-252, for a full exegesis of 1 Corinthians 11:10.

in public worship, a wife ought to wear a head covering upon her head "because of the angels."[31]

For many ancient communities female hair was the most prized public object of male desire and married women were to protect their hair from public view.[32] This context may explain the reference to both uncovered women and the angels. The uncovered women may become objects of male desire by opening themselves up to the possibility of sexual immorality, and hence it may *point back* to the fall of the Watchers. In 1 Corinthians 11:10 the object of the angels' interest is merely the uncovered women and not any lapses in worship on part of the men. The focus on merely uncovered women in public worship supports the view that Paul has the Watchers in mind.

One could paraphrase Paul as saying "remember the angels/Watchers and their fall." It may not be necessary to imagine that Paul thinks that the uncovered Corinthian Christian women are now vulnerable to the angels coming down and having sexual relations with them, thus repeating the fall of the Watchers.[33]

---

[31] One view is that the angels in 11:10 may refer to the holy angels who are guardians of public worship. However, there are no mention of angels, guardians of public worship, in other passages concerning public worship (11:17-34 and chapters 12-14), which makes this view unlikely. In addition, Paul may have a reason for using the definite article, "the angels," in 1 Corinthians 11:10 if he wants to stress that he is referring to a definite group of fallen angels: the Watchers.

[32] C.S. Keener, *1-2 Corinthians* (Cambridge: Cambridge University Press, 2005), 91-92.

[33] P.H. Alexander, "The Demonology of the Dead Sea Scrolls," in *The Dead Sea Scrolls after Fifty Years: A Comprehensive Assessment* (vol. 2; eds. P.W. Flint & J.C. VanderKam; Leiden: Brill, 1999), 351, plausibly argues that in the Dead Sea Scrolls demons are the spirits of the dead giants, and there is a close affinity between the view of demons in the scrolls and the NT, since in both demons are set within a strong theological framework. The use of the term "demons" in some early Jewish works designates a specific group of evil spirits – the spirits of the dead giants – who originate after the flood. In the *Book of* Watchers, the fathers of the giants (the sons of God/Watchers) do inspire the worship of false

Clearly, the angels here are personal beings. There may be a parallel with the sacrifices to the demons in 10:20f., since both 10:20 and 11:10 refer to the involvement of supernatural beings during worship (worship being an act that invokes spiritual beings).[34]

In support, one can add that Archie Wright notes that the violent behaviour of the giants is similar to the types of action by demons in Mark 1:23; 26; 5:2–8; 12; Luke 4:33–35; 8:29. Mark 5:4-5 may be influenced by the beliefs about the giants in *1 Enoch (Book of Watchers)*. In Mark 5 the possessed man's violent and destructive behaviour may be related to the demonic spirit's desire for a human body. That is, the demon seeks a human body (having previously had a human body) and now indwells it. [35] Further, the

---

gods before the flood, see my Relationship, pp.122-136 for a discussion. In the NT, this is expressed through the idea that the defeat of evil powers is a sign of the coming of the Kingdom of God. Further, in the gospels, demons are disembodied spirits (Matthew 12:43-45; Luke 11:24-26). The chief of the evil powers is Satan (Mark 3:22). Ultimately, evil powers will be punished (Matt 13:29). Given the above influences, it is therefore conceivable that Paul may be indebted to the same traditions and it is possible that the demons in 1 Corinthians 10:20f may be the spirits of the dead giants.

[34] P. Lampe, "Die dämonologischen Implikationen von 1 Korinther 8 und 10 vor dem Hintergrund paganer Zeugnisse," in *Demons: The Demonology of Israelite-Jewish and Early Christian Literature in Context of their Environment* (eds. A. Lange, H. Lichtenberger & K.F.D. Römheld; Tübingen: Mohr Siebeck, 2003), 596-597. Cf. Psalm 138:1; Luke 15:7; 10; 1 Timothy 5:21; Hebrews 1:6; 12:22f.

[35] Wright, *Origin*, 164, fn. 97; 221-222. Cf. P. G. Bolt, "Jesus, the Daimons, and the Dead" in *The Unseen World: Christian Reflections on Angels, Demons, and the Heavenly Realm* (ed. A.N.S. Lane; Carlisle: Paternoster, 1996), 75-102. Bolt says that (98-99) Jesus' confrontation with the demons in Mark shows links between the demons and the dead especially regarding the exorcism of the Gerasene demoniac in Mark 5:1-20. R. Bauckham, "Biblical Theology and the Problems of Monotheism," in *Out of Egypt: Biblical Theology and Biblical Interpretation* (ed. C. Bartholomew, M. Healy, K. Möller, & R. Parry; Milton Keynes/Grand Rapids: Paternoster/Zondervan, 2004), 222, fn. 96, also notes the connection between the demons and death. Bolt's conclusion that demons may be spirits of the dead coheres with my suggestion that the demons in 1 Corinthians 10:20f. may be the

Watchers and giants traditions are influential for the early church, since the early church fathers know the stories of the Watchers and giants. Thus, Justin Martyr (c. A.D. 161) asserts, in his *Second Apology*, 5.3–4, that the immoral gods of Greek mythology are, in reality, demons, the offspring of the angels who married human women.[36] Indeed, Tertullian does identify the angels of 1 Corinthians 11:10 with the Watchers in *On the Veiling of Virgins*, 7.

Given the above historical and literary context, it is therefore conceivable that Paul may be indebted to the same traditions and, very tentatively, the demons in 1 Corinthians 10:20f. may be the spirits of the dead giants.[37]

To sum up, the demons may be identified with the principalities and powers, the angels of the nations, and the spirits of the dead giants. The above three possibilities for the classification of the demons may not be exclusive options, but rather may be overlapping categories. There is no reason why the demons cannot be the spirits of the dead giants who have authority over the pagan nations and their cults, and "make up" the principalities and powers.[38] I shall explore the theological implications of the above classification in chapter 3.

---

spirits of the dead giants, and indeed is also consistent with Psalm 106:28, 37 that in the Psalm the demons are spirits of the dead.

[36] See also *Pseudo-Clementine Homilies*, 8:12-18; Tertullian, *Idol.* 4, *Apol.* 22; Commodianus, *Instructions* 3; Athenagoras, *Leg.* 25.

[37] Somerville discusses the possible classification of evil powers in 8:5b. First, Paul may be thinking of "angelic powers" who are mediators of divine rule. Secondly, they may be "invisible powers who keep themselves behind the rulers of the nations." Thirdly, they may be demons as in 10:20. Somerville, however, concludes that Paul is merely talking about the beliefs of the pagan world, for the pagans there are many gods and lords. R. Somerville, *La Première Épître de Paul aux Corinthiens* (vol. 2; Vaux-au-Seine: Editions de la Faculté de la Théologie Evangélique, 2005), 20-22.

[38] My thanks go to Dr. Thomas Renz for his stimulating questions regarding the identity and classification of the demons.

1.4. Conclusion

Paul defines an idol to be to the non-existent pagan god itself as well as the cult image. Paul in 1 Corinthians 10:18–20a focuses on the idolatry of *Israel* in history and the emptiness of idolatry. For Paul, the myths and beliefs in the pagan gods (as portrayed in Homer and Hesiod) are merely imaginary, lifeless, and false. Therefore, Zeus is an idol, and his cult image is also an idol, being spiritually lifeless. Idolatry is any act which involves participation in the honour or worship of an idol. Idolatry remains a danger, a threat, and a grievous sin for the church.

In 1 Corinthians 10:20–21 the demons are personal supernatural evil beings. The demons may be tentatively classified under the rubric of the principalities and powers, the angels of the nations, and, perhaps, the spirits of the dead giants (though other identifications are also possible). Therefore, idols and demons are two distinct entities. Idols are empty and spiritually lifeless. Demons are real spiritual evil personal beings.

Having explored the nature of idols/idolatry and the identity of the demons, the next chapter will consider the relationship between these two distinct entities.

2. The relationship between demons and idols in 1 Corinthians 10:18–22

> All the gods of the nations are idols: but our God made the heavens.
>
> OG 1 Chronicles 16:26[39]

> All the gods of the nations are demons: but the Lord made the heavens.
>
> OG Psalm 95 (96):5

1 Corinthians 10:18–22 raises the key questions of this study: How are real demons are related to lifeless idols? What is the nature of the relationship between demons and idols in 1 Corinthians 10:18–22?

Importantly, the arguments in chapter 1 imply that demons (who are real personal supernatural evil beings) and idols (which are unreal pagan gods and false and spiritually lifeless cult images) are two distinct, though associated, entities. Therefore, demons and idols *are not equated or strictly identified*, but are two distinct entities in relationship. The demon does not "inhabit" the cult image nor is the demon actually "present" within the cult image. Rather, demons and cult images are related or linked with one another in an arm's length relationship. Demons "stand behind" idols. This chapter will first present a translation of 1 Corinthians 10:18–22 and then examine three aspects of the relationship between demons and idols: the power of the demons, deception by the demons, and worship co-opted by the demons.

---

[39] My translation.

2.1. Extended Free Translation of 1 Corinthians 10:18–22[40]

[18] Consider the case of historical Israel's idolatry; are not all who eat the sacrifices common participants together in the food on the altar dedicated to an idol? [19] What then do I mean to affirm and imply? That food sacrificed to idols has any spiritual reality, or that an idol has any spiritual reality? [20] No, rather I imply that what they (the Israelites) sacrifice, "they sacrifice to demons, and also to what is not God," and I really do not want you Christians to become partners (with one another and with your pagan fellow–partners) in the sphere of the demons. [21] You Christians cannot drink from the cup belonging to the Lord Jesus Christ and the cup belonging to demons; you cannot corporately share in eating from the table belonging to the Lord Jesus Christ and the table belonging to demons. [22] Or what, are we in the process of provoking the Lord Jesus Christ to jealous anger? We are not stronger than the Lord Jesus Christ, are we?

2.2. The power of the demons

How precisely are the demons related to idols? First, the demons *are powerful and may enslave humanity into idolatry.* This power has three aspects. First, the power and rule of demons bring the worshippers into the sphere of influence or power of the *demons.* Demons, being supernatural beings, have spiritual power and authority. They may be the "gods" and "lords" in 1 Corinthians 8:5b, "just as there exist many 'gods' and many 'lords.'" Both titles, "gods" and "lords," imply their supernatural power and authority and stand in opposition to God the Father, and the Lord Jesus Christ in v. 6.

In 1 Corinthians 10:21 the opposition between Christ and the demons implies that the *daimonia* are powerful supernatural beings opposed to the lordship of Christ: "You cannot drink from the cup

---

[40] This free translation assumes the exegetical decisions made in this study. For a full exegesis, see chs. 4-5 of my, *Relationship.*

belonging to the Lord Jesus Christ and the cup belonging to demons; you cannot corporately share in the table belonging to the Lord and the table belonging to demons." To partake in the table of the demons is to offer the demons implicit allegiance and homage (cf. Revelation 9:20). In 10:20b Paul is passionately concerned that the Corinthians avoid participating in pagan sacrifices suggesting the power of the demons: "I do not want you Christians to be common partners in sacrifices to the demons." If the demons can be related to the powers and principalities, the angels of the nations, or the spirits of the dead giants, then these would be further indications of their power. Thus, idolaters do not intend to sacrifice to demons when they sacrifice to idols, but in doing so they serve the will and purposes of the demons (cf. Revelation 9:20; 13:4). Charles Hodge rightly comments that:

> Men of the world do not intend to serve Satan, when they break the laws of God in pursuit of the objects of their desire. Still in doing so, they are really obeying the will of the great adversary, yielding to his impulses, and fulfilling his designs ... to him all sin is an offering and homage. We are shut up to the necessity of worshipping God or Satan; for all refusing or neglecting to worship the true God, or giving to any other the worship that is due to him alone, is worshipping Satan and his angels. [41]

Thus, given Hodge's comment, the construction and worship of a cult image would ultimately serve the purposes of evil powers, even though the cult image itself is lifeless and has no spiritual reality. Therefore, pagan idolatry is a form of bondage exerted by the demons.

Secondly, there are parallels to the power of the demons in the Pauline corpus. Satan exerts formidable and dangerous spiritual power. Therefore, the demons exercise dominion and bondage over humanity's religions outside Christ. The demons may be under the

---

[41] C. Hodge, *The First Epistle to the Corinthians* (1857; repr., London: Banner of Truth, 1964), 193.

command of Satan and the demons may extend his power over the religions of the nations of the whole world (cf. Ephesians 2:1–3).

Thirdly, there is evidence in 1 Corinthians 10:6f. that Paul does refer to an evil inner desire in humanity to worship idols. Paul warns that the events of Israel's rebellion in the wilderness, which included idolatry, took place as warnings to Christians:

> And these things happened as examples for us so that we should not be those who desire evil things just as they desired evilly.

Paul's warning that Christians should not desire evil things just as Israel did probably has a reference to idolatry (cf. Numbers 11:34). Paul's warnings against evil desire and idolatry in vv. 6–7 suggest that the two are linked: there is an inner evil desire/inclination towards idolatry (cf. Romans 1:21–25; 2 Thessalonians 2:10; Ephesians 4:26f.). This inner evil desire is to have a god other than the true God to rule over them. The warning in 1 Corinthians 10:13, "no temptation has overtaken you that is not common to man" may be a warning against idolatry because of the context of Israel's idolatry of Israel (vv. 7–8) and Paul's exhortation against idolatry in v. 14, "therefore my beloved, flee from idolatry."[42]

The inner human desire to worship idols (Calvin says the human heart is "a factory of idols") suggests that idolatry is an addiction. We may believe that we are free and in control, like the alcoholic who insists that he is not addicted, but in reality we are enslaved by what we worship. Christians must flee idolatry as if it were a deadly disease.

To sum up, the demons' power means that they can enslave humanity into idolatry.

---

[42] A.T. Cheung, *Idol Food in Corinth: Jewish Background and Pauline Legacy* (Sheffield: Sheffield Academic Press, 1999), 146-147.

2.3. Deception by the demons

Secondly, the demons are related to idols because *these powerful demons deceive humanity into idolatry.* The deception of idolatry works in three ways. The first way is that demons deceive idolaters by inspiring them to believe in the spiritual reality of idols. This deception leads humanity astray and away from the true God. In 1 Timothy 4:1 (cf. Zechariah 13:2) the demonic spirits use human liars to lead people away from the truth of the gospel and by implication into error about God: "the Holy Spirit expressly says that in later times some will depart from the faith by devoting themselves to deceitful spirits and the teachings of demons." The relationship is drawn between the demonic spirits and false doctrine in 1 Timothy 4:1 and may imply that in 1 Corinthians 10:20 the demons deceive the Corinthian Christians into participation in idolatry.

In 1 Corinthians 10:20f. the deception inspired by demons may be a parody and counterfeit of spiritual truth and reality. The idols *appear* to be true deities, able to offer spiritual truth and life. Thus, demons may covertly inspire idolatrous notions in the minds of fallen humanity; these notions deceive and lead idolaters away from the gospel because of their sinful inner inclination. Evil powers may be able to influence some humans because of their inner evil inclination to idolatry.

Secondly, the idols (the cult images) themselves are deceptive in the same way that to believe that a copy is the real original is deceptive. A contemporary analogy would be the world of film which seems to be real but has the capacity to deceive those who believe that it is real. The idols seem to offer spiritual life and reality, and pagans do believe that the worship of their gods and their cult images corresponds with spiritual reality and brings them blessing. The cult images (considered in themselves) are merely material objects, devoid of spiritual life and reality. Therefore, idolatry is inherently deceptive for those who worship idols (see Romans 1:25 where idolaters exchange the truth about God for a lie).

The third way in which idolatry may be deceptive is that the demons may disguise themselves and appear to be real gods, worthy of worship. Volker Gäckle hints at the possibility when he says that in 1 Corinthians 10:19f. Paul still affirms the "vanity of the pagan gods, but he sees the power and the influence of demons behind their mask," and that Paul understands "the pagan gods and idols as a type of cover of the demonic powers."[43]

Building upon Gäckle's suggestions, it is possible that the idea behind the text (1 Corinthians 10:20f.) is that the demons change their forms into the gods of paganism and so deceive pagans into sacrifices to idols. There is support for this option in 2 Corinthians 11:14 where it is no wonder that false apostles can deceive because Satan masquerades as holy angel, "Satan transforms himself into angel of light."[44]

Therefore, the demons may assume the forms of the pagan gods who seem to offer spiritual life and reality. These disguises seem to be plausible but in fact are cloaks of the evil demons. Thus under this suggestion, Krishna, for example, seems to be a spiritually real and living god who will bring blessing if worshipped but it may be a fictitious role played by a demon in order to deceive the worshippers of Krishna. The cult image of Krishna may be the image of the disguise of a demon, and to worship Krishna's cult image would be to worship the cult image of a demon in disguise.

---

[43] V. Gäckle, *Die Starken und die Schwachen in Korinth und in Rom: zu Herkunft und Funktion der Antithese in 1 Kor 8,1-11,1 und in Röm 14,1-15,13* (Tübingen: Mohr Siebeck, 2004), 236, 238.

[44] Cf. Athenagoras, (c. 177), Leg. 26, says, "that it is the demons who act under their names [i.e. the pagan gods], is proved by the nature of their operations. For some castrate as Rhea; others wound and slaughter as Artemis; the Tauric goddess puts all strangers to death." And in 27, Athenagoras believes that the demons are "ever ready to lead men into error ... [to] take possession of their thoughts, cause to flow into their minds empty visions as if coming from the idols and statues" (translation from ANF 2.143) which implies that Athenagoras sees the *daimonia* as possibly being able to change their forms into pagan gods or at least appear to be gods to the pagans. He also states in Leg. 25 that the demons are the spirits of the dead giants. Cf. Pseudo-Clementine (4th century), Homilies 9.14f. (cf. 8.12f.), says that demons "appear in such forms as they please" and receive divine honours, and they appear in "the forms of the images" (translation from ANF, 8.277-288).

Under this possibility, the *daimonia*/demons can be equated with the many "gods" and "lords" in 1 Corinthians 8:5b, not in terms of their nature or essence, but in terms of the roles the demons adopt.

A contemporary analogy would be actors today adopting acting roles. Thus, we say "David Tennant is Doctor Who" meaning that Tennant plays the role of Doctor Who, a fictitious character in a TV series. Clearly, Tennant cannot be identified with Doctor Who in terms of his nature or personal identity. Alternatively, perhaps, spies who disguise themselves and assume fictitious identities in order to deceive their enemies would also be analogous. Therefore, the demons may try to achieve their aims into leading humanity (and Christians who participate in idolatry) away from God and Christ by disguising themselves as the pagan gods, and in these forms they deceive idolaters. Today it would mean that Allah, Buddha, etc. are fictitious roles played by demons in order to trick their worshippers into false worship.

Here 2 Corinthians 4:4 may provide illumination. In 2 Corinthians 4:4, the "god of this age" is Satan who influences and hinders unbelievers from receiving Paul's gospel. There is no deficiency in Paul's gospel. The deficiency of the unbelievers' rejection of the gospel lies in the work of Satan. In a blinded state, people may be ripe to be deceived by Satan appearing as an angel of light (cf. 2 Thessalonians 2:9ff). Possibly, the demons act overtly to enslave through an idolatrous evil desire and impulse. In this blinded state, humanity is deceived into believing in the spiritual life and reality of idols.

To sum up, demons deceive human beings into the worship of idols.

2.4. Worship co-opted by the demons

Thirdly, demons are related to idols because *the demons "stand behind" the idols and co-opt the worship consciously intended for the idols*. The "co-option" of sacrifices by the demons has six aspects that build on the exegetical arguments for demons and idols being distinct entities in chapter 1. First, the demons "co-opt" the sacrifices in the sense that they divert or use the sacrifices differently from that intended by the pagan worshippers. The demons "co-opt" the sacrifices by appropriating them as their own in order to bring pagan worshippers under their sphere of power or influence. Thus, Christophe Senft perceptively says:

> he [Paul] declares that behind the nothingness of the idols hide the demons, who are very real and who exploit to their profit the superstitious cult of the idolaters. So the pagans, by their cult empty of understanding (since the idols are nothing), render without knowledge to the demons a vile cult.[45]

Secondly, the demons are able to co-opt sacrifices since idolaters are deceived and deluded (they sacrifice to non-existent gods and mere physical images). For the pagan, the cult image is one of the manifestations of the god – sometimes his place of residence and sometimes a direct concentration of his powers. Therefore, an act performed on the cult image becomes an act upon the god itself.[46] Moshe Halbertal and Avishai Margalit stress that there is "a 'substitution' in idol worship of the symbol for the thing symbolized, in which some of the traits of the symbolized thing are transferred to the symbolizing thing."[47] The non-pagan fears that the cult image, by taking the place of God in the eyes of the idolater, thereby becomes "another god."[48]

Therefore, a cult image of a god is at the centre of the pagan's devotion, even if he may insist that the image is merely a

[45] C. Senft, *La Première Épître de Saint Paul aux Corinthiens* (Neuchâtel/Paris: Delachaux & Niestlé, 1979), 135. Bauckham, "Biblical Theology," 221, suggests that one possibility about the relationship between demons and idols exploit the fantasy of idolaters. B. Witherington, *Conflict and Community in Corinth: A Socio-Rhetorical Commentary on 1 and 2 Corinthians*, (Grand Rapids/Carlisle: Eerdmans/Paternoster, 1995), 197-198, says that while idols are not anything, nonetheless Paul believes that the demons who use them are something.

[46] M. Halbertal & A. Margalit, *Idolatry* (Cambridge/London: Harvard University Press, 1992), 40.

[47] Halbertal & Margalit, *Idolatry*, 40.

[48] Halbertal & Margalit, *Idolatry*, 40-41.

symbol of the god in the supernatural realm. Therefore, for a Hindu today, in theory, he may recognize the difference between the image of Krishna in the earthly shrine, and the god in heaven. Nevertheless, in practice, the revered and venerated cult image of Krishna becomes "another god."

Thus, for Paul, because the god *conceived by the pagans* is non-existent and the physical cultic image is spiritually lifeless, the demons can divert or co-opt the sacrifices intended for idols. So, indirectly, the demons receive the sacrifice intended for the pagan god. The idol is a counterfeit mediator unlike the true living mediator, Christ, who brings Christians to the true God. For Paul then, the demons do not reside within the idol, nor are idols an extension of the presence of demons, but they "stand behind" the idol and co-opt the sacrifices. Their influence is unrecognized by those participating in pagan sacrifices.

Thirdly, expanding on the previous point, it is sacrifices to, and the invocation of, idols that triggers the association of the demons with idols.[49] It is unlikely that the demons eat the sacrificial food or drink the blood or wine, there is no evidence in Paul that evil powers consume the sacrificial food and drink. The "co-optative" view therefore does *not* assume that the demons hover as unseen presences at pagan sacrifices, or that the pagan consciously worships demons. Rather the sacrifices mean that the worshippers come under the sphere of power or influence of demons. A contemporary analogy would be that the UK government's sphere of authority and power extends over all British citizens, even though

---

[49] Cf. Newton, *Deity*, 185-225. Newton (347) comments that some sacrifices were considered to be directed to the gods for thanking, honouring, seeking omens, purifying or averting evil and other sacrifices functioned as an offering to the dead or heroes to invoke their power or to honour them or as a sign of mourning, and the intended purpose of *thusia* was worship, veneration, honour, respect. Witherington notes that a Roman wanting to secure the good will of a god would make a vow, usually written on a tablet, and on the day of the sacrifice, he would attach the tablet to the statue of the god, and then pray facing the statue, lifting up his hands in supplication. B. Witherington, "Not so Idle Thoughts about *Eidolothuton*," *TynBul* 44 (1993), 24.

the government's physical presence is in central London.

Here the terminology of sacrifice is relevant. The terminology appears five times in three verses in 1 Corinthians 10:18–20. In v. 18, Paul asks his readers to consider Israel's eating the sacrifices as partners in the sacrifices upon the altar/place of *sacrifice*. In v. 19, sacrifice is present within the term, "food *sacrificed* to idol." In v. 20a, sacrifice appears twice "what they *sacrifice*, they *sacrifice* to demons and to what is not God". Newton rightly concludes that what "Paul clearly forbids is sacrifice by the believer."[50]

The terminology of sacrifice and idols implies that it is when idolaters pay allegiance to, invoke, call upon, and offer praise to idols through the offering of sacrifices that idolaters come under the influence of demons. Since the idols are spiritually lifeless and vehicles of deception, idols become media for demons, and the invocation of the idol during the sacrificial slaughter of the animal is co-opted by the demons. The invocation of the idol is the point at which idols become associated with demons. Therefore, idolaters unconsciously pay homage and allegiance to demons. Peter Lampe rightly says, "however, for Paul, hiding behind the pagan sacrificial cult are real existing demons, with contact made manifest through the sacrifice."[51]

However, there is no *direct relationship* or partnership established with demons. Rather, the recognition and invocation of an idol (which is a spiritual act) brings the participant under the sphere of influence of demons because the demons divert the invocation or prayer intended for the non-existent pagan god.[52]

The cult image itself is merely stone, wood, or metal. The image is not intrinsically related to evil powers, but only *becomes* a vehicle or medium for the influence of *daimonia* during the invocation of the deity. By extension, the sanctuary of an idol is not

---

[50] Newton, *Deity,* 368.
[51] Lampe, "Dämonologischen," 598.
[52] Gäckle, *Starken,* 238.

intrinsically associated with evil powers, and is only associated with evil powers at times of invocation and sacrifice.[53]

If the demons possibly disguise themselves as the pagan gods, then the invocation of Zeus (for example), would, in reality, invoke a demon disguised as Zeus, hence the demon is able to appropriate the invocation intended for Zeus. Here participants in sacrifices come morally under the influence of evil powers.[54] It is not that the idolaters offer sacrifices to demons in an intentional cultic act. Rather, the demons appropriate the sacrifices intended for idols by idolaters and so the idolaters come under the sphere of the power or influence of the demons in a spiritual sense, and in ethical terms idolaters can be counted within the domain of evil powers.

By "sphere of influence" I mean that the demons influence humans to worship false gods rather than the true God, and so the demons achieve their objective of keeping people in darkness. For idolaters to come under the "sphere of influence" of the demons does *not* mean that idolaters are "possessed" or indwelt by demons, or even that idolaters necessarily perform all sorts of wicked deeds. There is spiritual and ethical dualism here which seen in 1 Corinthians 10:21 "you cannot drink of the table of the Lord and the cup of demons. You cannot share in the table of the Lord and the table of demons."[55] Pagan sacrifices mean that the worshipper is placed in the domain of evil powers and is not in the domain of God/Christ.

---

[53] In 1 Corinthians 10:26 Paul cites Psalm 24:1, "the earth is the Lord's and its fullness," as allowing the purchase of food from the market, (which may be connected with the sale of meat from the idol temple), without investigation of its origins. In vv. 27-30 he allows (in some circumstances) attendance at private dinners, which implies that food *per se* is of no theological consequence.

[54] E.-B. Allo, *Saint Paul: Première Épître aux Corinthiens* (Paris: Gabalda, 1956), 244.

[55] Thiselton rightly says that the use of "you cannot" "conveys (i) a *logical* **cannot** (the two possibilities exclude each other); (ii) an *empirical* **cannot** (something will be destroyed if you try to do both); (iii) an *institutional* **cannot** (Christians cannot, and still be *counted* as "Christian")." A.T. Thiselton, *The First Epistle to the Corinthians: A Commentary on the Greek Text* (Grand Rapids/Carlisle: Eerdmans/Paternoster, 2000), 776.

Fourthly, the parallel of the Lord's Supper helps illuminate the relationship between demons and idols. Praise and homage of the true God in Christ in the Lord's Supper bring one under the sovereign power of God and the lordship of Christ (1 Corinthians 8:4b, 6; 10:16–17, 21; 11:23–26) – though in the Lord's Supper and in the invocation of God there is no co-option. The co-option of the sacrifices intended for idols by demons means that their strategy of leading idolaters away from God and Christ is successful. There is a supporting later reading from Cyril of Jerusalem (died 386). He says about 1 Corinthians 10:20 that, as at the Lord's Supper the bread and wine becomes the body and blood of Christ after the invocation, so "these foods [i.e. pagan sacrifices] of the pomp of Satan, though in their nature ordinary food, become profane through the invocation of evil spirits."[56]

Fifthly, Greg Beale's view of idolatry illuminates the co-option of sacrifices by demons. Beale perceptively says that just as the believer mirrors the character of the living God, it is likely that the idolater will reflect:

> The same dead spiritual attributes as the idols and the destructive and deceptive character of the demons that stand behind the idols. The idolaters inhabit the same unspiritual sphere and community as the demons. What one worships brings the worshipper into intimate contact with and under the powerful influence of the object of worship, whether the object is Christ or demons.[57]

Thus, the idolater constructs and manufactures an idol according to his own desires and by worshipping it will become, in character, as spiritually lifeless as the lifeless idol he worships and, ultimately, reflect the ungodly nature of the demonic realm (i.e. be opposed to the gospel of Christ).

---

[56] *Mystagogical Lecture* 1.7; Ambrosiaster (366-384), *Commentary on Paul's Epistles,* believes that, "Paul is saying that beneath the surface of the idol there is a demonic power which is out to corrupt faith in God," both cited in G. L. Bray ed., *1-2 Corinthians* (Downers Grove: IVP, 1999), 98.
[57] Beale, *We Become,* 230.

Sixthly, the motivation of the Corinthian "knowers" supports the "co-optative view." Outwardly the Corinthians do participate in idol feasts; they are perceived and seen to be involved, despite their unbelief in the spiritual reality of idols and their knowledge that "there is no God but one" (1 Corinthians 8:4). For Paul, the argument that the Corinthian "knowers" do not believe in idols is irrelevant, since the pagans intend to sacrifice to their gods but not to evil beings and nevertheless the demons co-opt the sacrifices. Crucially then, what applies to pagans also applies to the people of God.

Even if the Corinthian Christian "knowers" do not believe in pagan gods, even if they dismiss the god conceived by the pagan and the physical cultic image as an idol, a spiritually lifeless vanity, nevertheless by their outward participation in pagan sacrifices they ultimately participate, unknowingly, in sacrifices to demons.

Volker Gäckle notes, "because a demonic sphere of influence is already constituted by the purely formal invocation of the deity, also the Christian participating under a completely different motivation places himself under this sphere of influence."[58] Gäckle is right that the formal invocation of the deity triggers the *daimonic* sphere of influence and that the motivations of the Christian "knower" and of the pagan are different (the pagan believes in the spiritual reality of the idol while the Christian does not).

But, Gäckle misses the similarity between the pagan and Christian participant in the idolatrous sacrifices. Neither the pagan nor the Christian *intends* to sacrifice to demons, personal supernatural evil beings. The pagan and Christian participant are the same in their lack of consciousness and understanding that the *daimonia* co-opt the sacrifices.

Thus, the Christian who participates in sacrifices to demons excludes himself from Christ's sphere of influence, which makes it impossible to benefit from the Lord's Table (1 Corinthians 10:21).

---

[58] Gäckle, *Starken*, 238-239.

Therefore, the church by its communal participation in cultic sacrifice is deluded and deceived, like Israel in Deuteronomy 32:17, like the pagans, into sacrifices to demons, personal supernatural evil beings. Christians who come under the sphere of influence of demons provoke the jealous anger of Christ in v. 22: "Or are we provoking the Lord to jealous anger? We are not stronger than him are we?" The co-option of idol worship by the demons means that the demons achieve their purpose of leading people away from the domain of Christ.

2.5. Conclusion

The relationship between demons and idols can be called the "co-optative" view. It has three inter-locking aspects. First, the demons are powerful and enslave fallen humanity through humanity's inner evil inclination into idolatry. By doing the will of the demons, idolaters serve them. Secondly, the demons have the power to deceive humanity into worshipping idols because of the deceptive quality of idols; the demons inspire idolatry, and possibly change their forms by disguising themselves as the pagan gods. Thirdly, the demons deceive by "standing" or "hiding behind" the idols and co-opt and appropriate for their own use the sacrifices consciously offered to the idols. The recognition and invocation of an idol brings the worshipper under the sphere of influence of demons because the worshipper resembles the character of the idol and the demons divert the invocation or prayer intended for the idol. It means that the demons succeed in their objectives of keeping pagans from coming to Christ and the pagan becomes insensitive to the spiritual truth and reality of the gospel of Christ.

What then are the theological and pastoral implications for today of the relationship between demons and idols in 1 Corinthians 10:18–22? The final chapter will explore these implications.

3. The theological and pastoral implications of 1 Corinthians 8 and 10 for ministry today

> Christian doctrine ... functions, or should function as a set of protocols against idolatry.[59]
>
> Nicholas Lash
>
> Little children, keep yourselves from idols.
>
> 1 John 5:21

This chapter will reflect on the theological implications of the "co-optative" view of the relationship between demons and idols presented in the previous chapter. It will engage with the debate on "inclusivism," and, lastly, apply the findings of this study to some pastoral case studies which are of relevance for ministry today.

3.1. Theological reflections on the relationship between demons and idols

The "co-optative" view of the relationship between demons and idols, outlined in chapter 2, is theologically able to do justice to the seeming paradoxes and tensions that the idols are spiritually unreal and yet evil powers are real personal beings, and that pagans sacrifice to both vain idols and mighty evil powers.

We need to consider to the unique identity of the God of the Bible and its implication for the gods of other faiths. If *only* the Lord, the God of Israel, creates, rules, saves, and is wise, then Allah

---

[59] Cited in S.C. Barton, "Introduction," in *Idolatry: False Worship in the Bible, Early Judaism and Christianity* (ed. S.C. Barton; London: T & T Clark, 2007), 1.

does not really create or rule, Buddha really give wisdom, or Krishna really offer salvation (or any other god worshipped today). Here, in terms of theological reflection, the critique of the pagan gods may focus upon belief in the "wrong god." Halbertal and Margalit argue that for some Jews the right God can only be identified by his proper name.[60] Halbertal and Margalit say that the Jewish believer who thinks that the pagan's belief has no substance also believes that the referents of the names of the pagan's gods are empty.[61] Today it means that the names of Allah, Krishna, the gods of alternative spiritualities etc. are equally empty.

Thus, Paul has the following understanding of God, the pagan gods, idols, and evil powers. Firstly, the one true God has revealed himself in Christ. For Paul, the "one Lord, Jesus Christ" (1 Corinthians 8:6) is an eternal, self-existent holy being who solely creates, rules, saves, and judges. Secondly, the pagan gods are neither eternal nor self-existent and have no creative power nor can they save. Therefore, the pagan gods, *as conceived by the pagans as having creative power and the right to rule*, do not exist. For Paul, they are idols (1 Corinthians 8:4, 7).

Thirdly, Paul believes that idolaters ultimately worship evil powers (who do exist and are real) and these evil powers deceive their worshippers and may disguise themselves as the pagan gods and hence co-opt the worship intended for the pagan gods (1 Corinthians 10:20f; 2 Corinthians 11:14 cf. 2 Corinthians 6:14–16).

Fourthly, given the unique identity of God, Christian worship must be exclusive (1 Corinthians 8:6, 10:21).

Here is it worth considering the theological importance of the possibility that the demons who may "make up" the principalities and powers, are the angels of the nations, and are the spirits of the dead giants.

First, we need to reflect how entire political, social, and

---

[60] Halbertal & Margalit, *Idolatry*, 159.
[61] Halbertal & Margalit, *Idolatry*, 161.

religious structures can become idolatrous and demonic. These structures are susceptible to exploitation by the spiritual principalities and powers because the socio-political structures seem to defend and enhance life (through the provision of defence, law-and-order, health care, education, wealth creation, social justice etc.). Thus, we can be misled into thinking that our lives depend on these structures rather than on God our creator.

The key here is whether the structures are opposed to the preaching of the gospel. We live in an increasingly post-Christian society where it has become increasingly difficult not only to stand up for Biblical standards of morality and justice but also to witness to the uniqueness of Christ and the exclusiveness of the Christian faith. The structures of our society (and denominations) make it increasingly difficult to insist on evangelism, that only faith in Christ saves, and other faiths, however well intentioned, are ultimately mistaken. To insist that a person needs to convert is to face opposition and being called an intolerant bigot.

Yet the opposition to the exclusive nature of the gospel by our society may be a sign of the influence of principalities and powers of evil on our social and religious structures. Thus, it is possible for principalities and powers of evil to use heresy and hence influence even the structures of Christian denominations and churches (the super-apostles in 2 Corinthians 11:13ff. are servants of Satan masquerading as servants of righteousness).

Secondly, the spiritual reality of the angels of the nations/peoples standing behind different races and nationalities also needs theological understanding. It does not mean that we must place our energies into banishing so-called "territorial spirits" or exorcism, as many Pentecostals believe. We trust in an all-sovereign God who can use evil for good purposes (Job 1–2) and has conquered evil (Romans 8:38f.). We need not fear evil if we are walking with the Lord.

Yet, some Anglo-Saxon conservative evangelicals, like the Corinthian "knowers", may be blind to the spiritual reality of evil. Some conservative Anglo-Saxon evangelicals may believe in the supernatural world in theory, but in practice, God is the only supernatural being, and everything else belongs to the natural world. This view (perhaps being unconsciously influenced by Enlightenment rationalism) "excludes" the practical reality of the entire supernatural world of evil.[62] Here Christians coming from the cultures of Asia and Africa, which accept that the supernatural world influences the human world, are closer to the biblical worldview.

Therefore, we need to be aware that the angels of the nations may control particular peoples and communities so that they exhibit distinctive spiritual blindness. We need to understand each people group's particular spirituality, demolish strongholds and worldviews and take every thought captive to Christ (2 Corinthians 10:4f.) by putting on the full armour of God (Ephesians 6:10–20). The petition in the Lord's Prayer "deliver us from evil" must become real for us.

Thirdly, we need to consider the implications of the demons possibly being the spirits of the dead giants. At creation, God assigned human beings and angels to their own proper (holy) spheres. In some Jewish texts and possibly the NT as well, evil stems from a violation of God's separation of creation into different spheres: the angels/Watchers leave their heavenly domain and sphere for the domain of the earth and human beings and have sexual relations with human women. The mixing of angelic and human natures contravenes God's holy creation order into different spheres (in the same way that bestiality contravenes God's purposes). Evil is always de-creative and stems from rebellion against God's creation order. In Jewish traditions, the spirits of the dead giants are inherently evil because they are the offspring of a contravention of God's creation order; a confused and changed mixture of angelic and human natures. If holiness is a respect for God's separate spheres in creation, then unholiness is a violation of the separate spheres God has ordained at creation. Yet, the incarnation of Christ does not contravene creation order (since his

---

[62] See P.G. Heibert, "The Flaw of the Excluded Middle," *Missiology: An International Review* 10.1 (1982): 35-47.

two natures are without confusion, change, division, or separation). The incarnate Christ comes to restore creation and to bring redemption from the rejection of the creation order in idolatry. Idolatry and evil are de-creative while God in Christ is re-creative.

Further, the fact that the demons use idols fits with the nature of both idols and demons. Idols represent an unholy rebellion against God's creation order and are an exchange of the Creator for created things and the truth of God for a lie (Romans 1:21–25). In *1 Enoch,* demons are also products of a contravention of God's creation and deceive. It is therefore fitting that deceiving demons should use deceptive idols, created things, as weapons in their war against God's creation order by enslaving humanity into the worship of spiritually *dead* things. Pagans start to resemble the character of the gods they worship and reflect the opposition to the purposes of God which is inherent in the character of demons. On judgement day, God's fitting verdict on those who have worshipped spiritually *dead* things under the influence of demons/ the spirits of the *dead,* will be eternal spiritual *death* in hell.[63]

Therefore, given the above theological implications, Christians are warned both by Paul in 1 Corinthians 9–10 and by John in Revelation 9 against any participation in idolatry. Importantly, Revelation 9:20 warns Christians against any compromise with idolatry when it states that, despite plagues, idolaters, "did not repent of the works of their hands, so as to stop paying homage to demons, and the idols of gold, silver, bronze, stone, and wood – which cannot see or hear or walk." Beale's conclusions about the relationship between demons and idols in Revelation 9:20f. are relevant to Paul, that:

---

[63] Further, the relationship between demons and idols is a contrasting parallel of Paul's view of true worship. Just as Christ is a true and living mediator who brings believers to worship a holy spiritual being, God, and to reflect his character, so the idol is a false and lifeless mediator which brings those who are involved in pagan rites to worship unholy spiritual beings, demons, and to reflect their opposition to the gospel of Christ.

Horrible demons stand behind the idols ... [and] idols are the tools employed by demons to keep people under the anaesthetic effects of spiritual ignorance. The gruesome parabolic description of the demons is intended to shock the true people of God out of their complacent condition, as they realize what spiritual spectres really lurk behind the idols.[64]

Christians today may be tempted to compromise by joining the worship of other faiths. The stark antitheses and exclusivity present in 1 Corinthians 10:21 imply that there is no middle way between true worship of God and worship of evil powers.

It is a devastating response to the Corinthian "knowers'" position. Outwardly, the Corinthians are seen to join with pagans in the worship of pagan gods. Idolatry is not neutral nor is participation in idol feasts for social purposes an intermediate position between Christian worship and worship of false gods. Rather, Paul exhorts the Corinthian "knowers" (and any Christian "knowers" today!) not to participate in pagan meals because it means that the sacrifices are ultimately to evil spiritual beings. Participation in pagan meals means ultimately to be partners in sacrifices to evil spiritual beings.

The "knowers'" objection that they do not believe in pagan gods and are in no danger is met by Paul's agreement that the pagan gods do not exist and yet evil beings are the ultimate objects of the sacrifices. Pagans intend to worship Allah, Krishna, Buddha, and other non-existent gods, and do not intend to sacrifice to evil spiritual beings. Despite the pagans' good intentions, demons are the ultimate objects of worship to idols.

Crucially, Israel, in Scripture, were partners with pagans in their idol feasts and despite the intentions of the Israelites they ended up sacrificing to evil powers: "they sacrifice to demons and to

---

[64] G.K. Beale, *The Book of Revelation* (Grand Rapids/Carlisle: Eerdmans/Paternoster, 1999), 520. Further, Beale, *We Become*, 261, sees in both 1 Corinthians 10:20 and Revelation 9:20 that the idolater becomes identified with the idol and its demonic character.

what is not God." The Christian, in Corinth and today, must not repeat the mistake of the ancient people of God. If they continue to participate in other faiths, they will rouse the jealous anger and strength of Christ.

Thus, the non-existence of pagan gods and unbelief in them make no difference to the horrifying reality: that participation in idol feasts means participation in the sphere of evil spiritual beings. Paul's argument considerably raises the stakes and makes participation in idol feasts sinful and evil. *This is the key and heart* of Paul's response to the Corinthian "knowers," and an important part of his theological framework about idolatry. Idolatry for Paul is still abhorrent and still brings the wrath of God upon the people of God who participate in it. The ultimate reason for this abhorrence is that personal supernatural evil beings stand behind idols. In this sense, God's attitude towards idolatry is unchanged.

To sum up, the uniqueness and exclusiveness of the one true and living God means that true worship must also be exclusive. Evil powers operate through political, social, and religious structures. Evil is fundamentally a rebellion against God's creation order. Scripture warns Christians against any compromise with idolatry.

3.2.   *Theological implications for the debate on 'inclusivism'*

If idolatry is still abhorrent to God, then what is the theological status of other faiths today? There is perhaps no more important political and social issue today than that of the relationship between different faiths in a world of many different religions. It is also a central issue in Christian theology and praxis.

One answer that tries to uphold the demands of gospel with sensitivity to other faiths is that of Christian world religions inclusivism.[65] This view maintains that while God has revealed himself in Jesus Christ and he is central to salvation, nevertheless salvation itself is available in other religions. Those of other faiths, like Islam, Hinduism, Buddhism, etc. are "included" in Christ. The person faithfully committed to the practice of his religion is touched by grace and hence is, in Karl Rahner's famous phrase, an "anonymous Christian." While the church is the primary mode of salvation, nevertheless God may use elements in other faiths as means of grace. Therefore, other faiths are sufficient, though imperfect, means of God bringing people to saving faith.[66] World religions inclusivists make six key points.[67]

First, Clark Pinnock criticizes scholars who have no personal experience of people of other faiths. Pinnock is right that any Christian theology worthy of its name must engage with the reality of millions of people around the world (and in the UK) of different faiths.[68] Nevertheless, Christian theology and world religions inclusivists must also reckon with the experience of those, like myself, who come to Christ from other faiths.

Many of those who come to Christ from other faiths have found that from their Christian perspective what is lacking in their previous religion is, quite simply, a right relationship with God and salvation. The question posed by those who have converted from other faiths is whether their experience of moving from being under the wrath of God in their previous faith to now being at peace with

---

[65] This position is slightly different from "general revelation inclusivism," see C.W. Morgan, "Inclusivisms and Exclusivism" in *Faith Comes by Hearing: A Response to Inclusivism* (ed. C.W. Morgan & R.A. Peterson; Downers Grove/Nottingham: IVP/Apollos, 2008), 32-34.

[66] Morgan, "Inclusivisms and Exclusivisms," 32-33.

[67] In this section, I engage with the views of Clark Pinnock as my debate partner because of his importance, and as representative of the world religions inclusivist view. For views of other world religions inclusivists, see the essays by Gerald McDermott, Amos Young, and Miriam Adney in *No Other Gods before Me?: Evangelicals and the Challenge of World Religions* (ed. J.G. Stackhouse: Grand Rapids: Baker, 2001).

[68] C. Pinnock, "Inclusivist View," in *Four Views on Salvation in a Pluralistic World* (ed. D.L. Okholm & T.R. Phillips; Grand Rapids: Zondervan, 1996), 107.

God is theologically true. Thus, I was, according to the tenets and practices of Zoroastrianism, a faithful Zoroastrian. I went to the fire temple, believed, and practiced the central injunctions of the faith. According to world religions inclusivists, the grace of the true God touched me even if I did not have the fullness of understanding about Christ. Thus, for world religions inclusivists, when I became a Christian what happened was that my understanding and experience of God became fuller, not that I moved from being in a wrong relationship with God to being in right relationship with God.

Therefore, the world religions inclusivist view ignores the actual experience of people like myself who believe that we moved from judgement to salvation when we became Christians. It also ignores the experience of the Philippian jailer who asks Paul "what must I do to be saved?" and receives the answer "believe on the Lord Jesus Christ and you will be saved" (Acts 16:30f.), implying that conversion for the jailer *was* an experience of salvation. The point that pagans need to convert to the true and living God to be saved is further made in Acts 14:15 and 17:30 when Paul urges the pagans of Lystra and Athens to reject idolatry, while in 1 Thessalonians 1:9f. he commends the Thessalonians for turning from idols to a true and living God.[69]

Secondly, inclusivists often cite the cases of "pagan saints" (Melchizedek, Jethro etc) and especially the Roman centurion Cornelius in Acts 10 as evidence that those of other faiths are in right relationship with God. Pinnock says that God was present in Cornelius' religion since he was a non-Christian and a Gentile and yet was God-fearing.[70] However, this view ignores the fact that Cornelius understood the OT Scriptures, being a God-fearer (Acts 10:2). The story of Cornelius portrays a salvation–historical shift and shows that the coming of the Holy Spirit at Pentecost means that salvation is now open to all Gentiles who repent. Most importantly,

---

[69] See E.K. Schnabel, "Other Religions: Saving or Secular?" in *Faith Comes by Hearing: A Response to Inclusivism* (ed. C.W. Morgan & R.A. Peterson; Downers Grove/Nottingham: IVP/Apollos, 2008), 98-122.
[70] Pinnock, "Inclusivist View," 109.

Cornelius still needed to believe in Christ to be forgiven (Acts 10:42f.) and he himself affirms that it is through Peter's proclamation about Christ that he is saved (Acts 11:14).

Thirdly, Pinnock maintains that God makes positive use of other faiths when he says:

> I welcome the Saiva Siddhanta literature of Hinduism, which celebrates a personal God of love, and the emphasis on grace that I see in the Japanese Shin-Shu Amida sect. I also respect the Buddha as a righteous man (Matthew 10:41) and Mohammed as a prophet figure in the style of the Old Testament.[71]

Pinnock warmly approves of the story in C.S. Lewis' *The Last Battle* in which the pagan soldier Emeth learns to his surprise that Aslan (a great righteous lion symbolizing Christ) regards his worship of the pagan god, Tash, as ultimately directed to Aslan and as being truly worship of himself.[72] Thus, in Lewis' narrative, Aslan tells Emeth:

> I take to me the services thou hast done to him [Tash] ... If any man swear by Tash and keep his oath for the oath's sake, it is by me that he has truly sworn, though he know it not, and it is I who reward him ... For all find what they truly seek.[73]

Therefore, for Pinnock and Lewis, the worship of other faiths when done with the intention to seek truth is "co-opted" by God in Christ as being true worship.

Importantly, Paul, in line with the Biblical witness, counters with another sort of "inclusivism." Yet, Paul would assert that the worship of other faiths is, in fact, "co-opted" by evil powers and so worshippers are "included" in their sphere of influence. For Paul, the gods of other faiths, as conceived by other faiths, are merely

---

[71] Pinnock, "Inclusivist View," 110.
[72] Pinnock, "Inclusivist View," 107.
[73] C.S. Lewis, *The Last Battle. The Chronicles of Narnia* (London: Collins, 1980), 155.

fictional creations; they do not exist. Since Paul believes both that the gods, as conceived by pagans, are non-existent, and cult images are spiritually lifeless, the point would apply to those faiths (like Islam) that do not use physical cult images in their worship. For Paul, and the OT, the gods of other faiths are merely the creations of the human mind which are used by evil powers for their nefarious purposes. However, the gospel is the revelation of the true God and therefore not a human creation or construction (Romans 1:16f.; 1 Thessalonians 2:13).

Fourthly, Pinnock does recognize that evil forces can influence all religions. He does believe that all religions can contain terrible errors and lead to horrible atrocities. He recognizes that religions can be used by the fallen powers of this age. Pinnock says that, "witchcraft and Nazism are not valid responses to the divine, according to the gospel."[74] However, Pinnock misunderstands the nature of the erroneous and demonic aspects of religions. Paul's point in 1 Corinthians 10:20f. is *not* that some gross forms of idolatry (like Satanism and witchcraft) are demonic. Rather, crucially, Paul's point is that *all* other faiths are *always* idolatrous, and are exploited by demons.

Other faiths are inherently tainted by error and evil. In the terms of Lewis' story, the worship of Tash is "co-opted" by the White Witch who deceives the worshippers of Tash and worship is ultimately rendered to her. It is not that Tash is a type of Christ but rather Tash is a type of the anti-Christ. For Paul, there is no middle way between the worship of the true and living God through Christ and the worship of evil powers through other gods.

Paul's point in 1 Corinthians 10 is not that some particularly reprehensible practices of some faiths are demonic or that some pagans are immoral, demon-possessed, or inhabited by demons. Paul does not believe that demons eat the sacrifices offered to idols and hence the food is "contaminated" or even that demons are locally present during pagan worship. Rather, Paul's point is a

---

[74] Pinnock, "Inclusivist View," 113.

theological one; that *all* the worship of *all* other faiths is ultimately "co-opted" by demons, despite the good intentions of the worshippers. It means that those of other faiths come under the sphere of influence of evil powers, which keeps people from coming to Christ (and therefore is evil).

The errors of a visible church and the sins of professing Christians do mean that a church may be susceptible to idolatry and evil (1 Corinthians 10:6–11, 20; Ephesians 4:26f.; 1 John 3:10, 4:2–6, 5:21). Nevertheless, the true church is not *inherently and essentially* idolatrous and corrupt because it has the gospel.[75]

Fifthly, world religions inclusivists respond by arguing that other religions preserve elements of the goodness of general revelation and therefore one cannot dismiss other faiths as merely demonic.[76] This is true; when I was a Zoroastrian I understood something about the goodness of divinity, creation, morality, the need for ceremonial purity and sacrifice. One can agree with Pinnock that the Saiva Siddhanta literature of Hinduism contains elements of divine love; that Amida Buddha emphasizes grace, and that Mohammed is a prophetic figure.

However, crucially, the idolatrous and, ultimately, demonic worship of other faiths does not mean a repudiation of general revelation. Rather, my "co-optative" view argues that idols *appear* to offer spiritual truth and reality and that *lies* and *deception* are central to the strategy of evil powers. Note here that Paul calls idolatry "*the* lie" (*tō pseudei*) in Romans 1:25 (i.e. idolatry is the big lie). Jesus, in John 8:44, associates evil with lies when he calls the

---

[75] Therefore, it is possible for a visible church and professing Christians to become idolatrous and come under the sphere of power of evil. The possibility of an idolatrous church raises the question as to when a visible church actually forsakes its claim to be a true church. Article 19 of the Anglican 39 Articles states that a true visible church is a congregation of faithful men in which the Word of God is purely preached and the sacraments duly administered. The current debate in the Anglican Communion is, for some, a debate whether the TEC has so compromised the gospel and hence its claim to be a true church.

[76] Pinnock, "Inclusivist View," 117-118.

devil "a liar" because he is by nature a liar, and also "the father of lies" who authors and inspires lies. Jesus maintains that the devil was a "murderer from the beginning" which implies the devil causes spiritual death through his lies. Here, Jesus may be alluding to Genesis 3:1–13 and the serpent's deception of Eve given the reference to the devil being a "murderer from the beginning."

If lies and deception are central to the strategy of evil powers, then an idol may appear to be a medium of divine revelation, presence, and love but is ultimately spiritually unreal. Further, the deception by demons through idols depends on some elements of general revelation (and possibly special revelation given that the Noahide covenant is made with all humanity) being preserved in other faiths. Both the idols and the demons must *appear* to be attractive and to be trustworthy in order to deceive successfully. Thus, a successful strategy of deception must preserve an element of truth in order to appear attractive and to be accepted.

Therefore, idolatry is a parody of true worship, since in 1 Corinthians 10:21 the table of demons and the table of the Lord are contrasted. The table of demons mimics the table of the Lord.[77] Indeed, evil powers must conceal themselves and be counterfeits in order to pervert and corrupt. Thus, just as counterfeit pound notes look like the real thing but are subtly different and fool many people, so pagans are fooled by idolatry into believing that their faith is real worship of the true God but, in reality, idolatry is worship of false gods.

Further, evil powers are hypocrites; Satan masquerades as an angel of light (2 Corinthians 11:14). The goal of demonic deception is corrupt – to lead people away from faith in Christ and hence salvation. If people are kept in the lie of idolatry and from saving faith in Christ then the strategy of the powers of darkness has succeeded. Evil (and hence evil powers' "co-option" of pagan

---

[77] See M.J. Ovey, "Idolatry and Spiritual Parody: Counterfeit Faiths," *Cambridge Papers* 11.1 (2002) 1-10 and N.T. Wright, "One God, One Lord, One People: Incarnational Christology for a Church in a Pagan Environment," *ExAud* 7 (1991): 52-53.

worship) must be defined theologically and christologically. We can define evil as "opposition to the true God's holy and righteous will and purposes in Christ." The purpose of evil powers is to keep people in idolatry.

Sixthly, Pinnock argues while the beliefs of other faiths may be false, authentic faith and holy actions may flow from persons of other faiths.[78] For world religions inclusivists, the worship of other faiths simply does not mean that all their worship is demonic, or that worshippers are "demon possessed," or involved in terrible evil behaviour (such as murder or child abuse). But, in my "co-optative view," the ultimately demonic worship of other faiths does not necessarily mean that demons inhabit the images of pagan gods, or are present at pagan worship, or that worshippers are demon possessed. Neither does it mean that pagans will necessarily commit sexual immorality or murder or such sins.[79]

Idolaters may be well-intentioned; they seek after spiritual reality but they are cruelly deceived. They have "faith," but their faith is a "false faith." The evil powers then anaesthetize those of other faiths to the destructive consequences of their idolatry, they do not realize that their worship is idolatrous and sinful, and thus are desensitised to the claims of Christ. Therefore, the proper

---

[78] Pinnock, "Inclusivist View," 118.

[79] Sometimes the worship of other faiths does involve both sexual immorality and murder. Psalm 106:37 describes the gruesome sacrifices of children to demons. In India, there have been periodic stories of the sacrifice of children to the goddess Kali. Even in these chilling cases, deception operates. The idolaters who sacrifice children genuinely believe that child sacrifices will make the gods propitious to their needs for healing etc. These pagan sacrifices are parodies of the true and willing self-sacrifice of the Son to the Father which truly propitiates God (Romans 8:3). Sexual immorality (both actual and metaphorical) can also be associated with idolatry (1 Corinthians 10:7f.) and mimics the true marriage between Christ and the church. Cultic prostitution has been a feature of some Hindu worship (cf. the *Kama Sutra*). There is a conceptual association between sexual immorality and idolatry since both sex and worship seem to be life-giving and offer profound and joyful experiences.

evangelical response to those of other faiths is pray for them (that Christ may release them from spiritual bondage), to love those of other faiths, and evangelize them.

Further, Beale's thesis, that we resemble what we revere, either for ruin or for destruction, raises very important implications: that worshippers may reflect the character of the one(s) they worship. Thus, Muslims may tend to resemble the remote, strict, and impersonal Allah they worship. Hindus may become as insensitive to spiritual reality as their spiritually unreal gods. Secularists may become greedy, arrogant, and addicted to pleasure because they resemble their ultimate values of money (cf. Ephesians 5:5, Colossians 3:5), power, and sexual fulfilment. Christians may become more like the righteous and gracious character of Jesus.

To sum up, the ultimately demonic nature of the worship of other faiths strongly supports the doctrine of the uniqueness of Christ and the exclusive nature of the Christian faith for salvation, and undermines world religions inclusivism.

3.3.   Pastoral Case Studies

Having considered the theological implications of other faiths, we now need to consider how we can apply these theological principles pastorally. I have based the case studies below on my real experiences. Christians round the world face these sorts of issues on an everyday basis. The key principles are love and truth. We need to be winsome and gentle, yet also clear in applying the Biblical injunctions.

1. You are a local minister and have been invited to an inter-faith event to pray for world peace. The representatives of all the major Christian denominations will be present, as will representatives from the Hindu, Muslim, and Sikh communities. An evangelical friend calls you up saying that he is going because it is an opportunity to make contact with other faith leaders and may result in future evangelistic opportunities. The same week you receive a letter inviting you to an inter-faith "dialogue". Do you go to both events, one, or none?

We may commend our evangelical brother's keenness to make contact with those of other faiths. We do need to take opportunities to present the gospel to people of other faiths.

While an inter-faith prayer meeting is not quite the same as participating in the normal worship service of another faith, there would nevertheless be an opportunity to participate in the prayers of other faiths. Therefore, attendance at the inter-faith prayer gathering may be unwise. No doubt, one could go and not participate in the prayers. Yet, the representatives of the other faiths would still assume that your attendance implies an acceptance of the tenets of their faith. Thus, even attendance would compromise any evangelistic witness and give the wrong impression of the gospel to other faith leaders. Better simply to phone up other faith leaders and arrange to meet up. Explain to your evangelical friend the meaning of 1 Corinthians 10 and advise him not to go either.

As for the inter-faith "dialogue," it depends on whether it is going to be a genuinely open discussion. In my experience, the implicit assumption is that inter-faith "dialogue" means that all faiths are equal and that no-one (especially a Christian) should claim that their faith is better or unique. You could write back saying that you can only attend if you are allowed genuinely to debate the uniqueness of Christ and the exclusivity of the gospel.

On a personal note, the inter-faith deanery chapter meeting in Wolverhampton that I attended (but did not participate in) was odd. All of us who attended were Anglican clergy. Nobody from another faith was present. Yet we were led through the Scripture readings and prayers of different faiths. The implicit theological assumption of the organizers seems to have been that all faiths (including the Christian one) were provisional and incomplete attempts by human beings to reach God. All faiths were somehow vehicles of God's grace. For them, idolatry taints all faiths (including Christianity). The organizers believed that Christ was special and Christianity was their personal preference, but Anglican clergy should be "open" to learning about God from different faiths, especially in a multi-faith city like Wolverhampton.

It did not occur to the organizers that in their attempt to be "inclusive" and "open" they dismayed conservative evangelicals. I was saddened since their theological presuppositions implied that the considerable personal sacrifices I made in converting from Zoroastrianism were in vain (at least regarding my salvation before God).

Further, the organizers seem to have failed to recognize that this meeting was a betrayal of their ordination vows and, above all, offensive to their Lord to whom they professed allegiance and arouses his jealous anger (1 Corinthians 10:22). Here the biblical concept of harlotry is an important consideration (cf. Exodus 34:13).[80] The Church is married to its Lord (Ephesians 5:25–33). To be involved with another the lord of another faith is to commit spiritual adultery. The image is distasteful and shocking, but the Bible uses the image to shock us out of our complacency, and show us just how sinful the Lord considers participation in the worship of other lords to be.

---

[80] See R.C. Ortlund, *Whoredom: God's Unfaithful Wife in Biblical Theology* (NSBT 2; Leicester: Apollos, 1996), 25-46.

These sorts of pastoral hard cases may be what Paul has in mind in 1 Corinthians 8–10. The Corinthian Christians participated in idol feasts not because they believed in idols but because of the social pressures placed on them to participate. They justified their participation on the basis of the emptiness of idolatry (1 Corinthians 8:4) and Christian "rights" and "freedom" in indifferent matters such as eating food offered to idols in the pagan temple (1 Corinthians 8:9; 10:23; 29b). Paul's answer to these hard cases is clear: no participation whatsoever in idol feasts, rather flee from them (1 Corinthians 10:14)!

First, we need to love the first brother. We need to understand the pain this converted Hindu feels at the death of his father. He needs your friendship, prayers, and love. Those converted from other faiths feel that they have lost their identity and culture. They need love from the church family.

He should continue to love his family and comfort his mother and relatives. He can welcome mourners to the family home and make arrangements for refreshments.

Yet, you should gently say that Christian "freedom" is not the issue here: this a salvation issue. His intentions and beliefs, that he does not intend to worship the Hindu gods and does not believe in them, are not strictly relevant here. However, you need, very compassionately, to explain to the Christian from a Hindu background the ultimately demonic nature of Hindu worship.

What matters is whether the family intends the funeral to be an act of Hindu worship. He should not participate in any Hindu ceremony which has a religious character. He should hand over his duties to a younger brother. He should respect his father's memory in another way (like sending some money to a charity). He can go to the crematorium for the cremation, though not to participate in any religious ritual. This is hard teaching, and you need to explain it with pastoral sensitivity.

The case of Chinese ancestor reverence is even more complex. Again, this Chinese Christian needs your support and love. We need to understand that, for a Chinese person, respect for family elders is very important. Even though in Chinese Tao religion, the ancestors are not exactly "gods," nevertheless one is still offering them a reverence and service that should only be offered to the Trinity.

In Numbers 25:1-3 and Psalm 106:28 Israel is condemned for participating in sacrifices to Baal Peor, a cult which most probably involved eating sacrifices offered to the spirits of the dead.[81] In the NT, the verbs *proskuneō* and *latreuō* (usually translated by "worship") and used in relation to God and idols have the sense of "pay homage/allegiance" and "religious/cultic service." John forbids Christians to offer any sort of cultic homage to the Roman emperor cult (which involved offerings to both living and dead members of the Imperial family) in Revelation 13-14 as ultimately involving homage paid to the first beast/Satan. Further, Paul, in Romans 1:25, is horrified by any service given to the creature rather than the creator.[82]

---

[81] See my *Relationship*, 102-107, 169-175, for exegesis of these passages.

[82] Cf. the ban on necromancy in Deuteronomy 18:9-13 and the ban on paying homage to angels in Colossians 2:18; Revelation 22:8f.

So, the NT bans any Christian involvement and participation in the ceremonies of any other faith. Therefore, the Chinese student should be gently guided not to participate in reverence of his ancestors.

On a personal note, this is my practice. I love my family, and understand their culture. I do attend coming-of-age ceremonies (Navjotes), weddings, and funerals of my Zoroastrian family. These religious rites of passage are not held in Zoroastrian fire-temples (from which non-Zoroastrians are barred) but in the temple courtyards. I do not wear any cap (which is worn when prayers and worship are conducted) because that is a sign of participation. For the same reason, I do not say any prayers or make a sandalwood offering to the fire.[83] In addition, I do not eat any of the fruit that has been dedicated to Ahura Mazda (the Zoroastrian chief god) which is then eaten by worshippers after the priests have finished reciting the liturgy.[84] My principle is: love, attend, but do not participate.

---

[83] In Zoroastrianism, a "sacred fire" is the key medium of the presence of the chief god, Ahura Mazda.

[84] There are cases I know of where Christians from Hindu backgrounds have been forced by their families into temples and feel very uncomfortable at having been forced into the idol temple. Here, clearly, the Christians forced into the temples are not sinning. The case of Naaman in 2 Kings 5:17ff. is similar. Naaman recognizes the sinfulness of idolatry, accompanies his king into the temple and feels uncomfortable at the king using his arm to bow to the idol in the temple.

> *3. A lovely Sikh family move in next door to you. You get to know them socially. One day the father comes to visit you and says that his daughter has just got engaged and that he would be honoured if you would grace the occasion of his beloved daughter's wedding at the temple and at the subsequent reception. Would you go? Would your answer be any different if a Sikh man has come to church recently, is interested, and may have made some sort of a commitment to Christ?*

In this pastoral case, 1 Corinthians 8:7–13 is important. Verse 7 is the important verse. Paul says:

> But, not in all (is) this knowledge, some because of their relationship [or custom] until now with the idol, eat food as if offered to an idol, and their self-awareness [or conscience] being weak, is defiled.

Importantly, the former pagan eats food here *as if* it has truly been offered to the idol. It is likely that Paul is describing the former pagan's relationship with a particular god (i.e. the "weak" person still thinks that the god, Zeus, whom he used to worship is a divine being). The phrase implies that former pagans believe that offerings are made both to the god itself and to the cult image of the god as an extension of the god's presence and endowed with spiritual reality.[85]

The man's self-awareness (or conscience) is defiled not because he feels offended and is sensitive about eating idol food because he has been led into eating by the example of some Christian "knowers." Rather, Paul's point is that this man (who lacks knowledge about the non-existence of pagan gods) still believes in the existence of pagan gods. Therefore a new convert can be led back into his previous idolatry; a sin so serious that it would lead to him being defiled before God and would lead to the loss of his salvation. Paul's point is to insist that he would give up all his rights (v. 13) if it would prevent someone from being destroyed by idolatry.

---

[85] G.W. Dawes, "The Danger of Idolatry: First Corinthians 8:7-13," *CBQ* 58 (1996): 89.

Paul concedes that, in abstract conceptual terms, Christians have the social "right" to enter and participate in idol feasts; their culture and society allows them this right (v.9). Indeed, food, merely considered as food, is a morally neutral and indifferent matter (v.8). Food *as food* is not contaminated or harmful (1 Corinthians 10:19). Food as food is clean (10:25 cf. Mark 7:19). However, this "right" to eat in idol temples should not be used because it may lead to the loss of salvation of a brother.

The importance of this discussion is that 8:7–13 cannot be used to establish the practice of eating food offered to idols and participating in the worship of other faiths today as a the exercise of Christian "freedom" in a morally neutral matter (provided it does not offend another brother or sister).

Attendance at the Sikh temple requires a level of participation (such as covering your head when worship takes place). The issue of wearing a head covering in a Sikh temple is rather like the eating of food in the idol temple in 1 Corinthians 8:7–13. Food, when it is central to pagan worship, is never merely food but involves participation in idolatry (1 Corinthians 10:7; 10:20f.). Thus, it is not possible to go to the Sikh wedding since it requires a level of participation (a head covering) of all who attend.

If someone from a Sikh background may have made a commitment to Christ in your church, then it is probably better to skip the wedding reception as well. A possible new believer should face these obstacles. For a newly professing Christian from a Sikh background to return to the temple because of your example would defile their right standing before God and be tragic (1 Corinthians 8:7–13).

Indeed, in Wolverhampton, I once met a man from a Sikh background who said that he had made a commitment to Christ, but still believed that the Sikh god was also divine. I gently told him that while the intentions of other faiths are honourable, nevertheless, other faiths are ultimately false and he should not participate in Sikh worship again. If I had been observed by him in the Sikh temple near to my church, my example would have been catastrophic.

> *4. A great new Indian restaurant has opened up in the area. It is run by Muslims. Do you inquire whether the meat in the restaurant is Halal or not? On a subsequent visit, you see that the menu announces that only Halal meat is used in the restaurant. Do you eat?*

The answer is that you do not inquire whether the meat is Halal. Paul in 1 Corinthians 10:25f. says that no investigation of the origin of the meat purchased in the Corinthian marketplace needs to be made since (citing Psalm 24:1), "the earth is the Lord's and all its fullness." If a pagan is unconcerned about the origin of the food, then a Christian should not be concerned either because food as food is a gift of God in Christ.

If a pagan indentifies the food then the question becomes trickier. Once more, the key issue is the *intention* of the pagan. In the case of Halal food, it is not as if the cooks who use Halal meat in cooking intend its eating to be an act of worship; they use Halal meat because it has come from a clean animal and been killed according to Muslim regulations. Therefore, it is acceptable to eat Halal meat.

While the origin of Halal meat is idolatrous (since Muslim prayers would have been spoken at the time of the killing of the animal) so was at least some of the meat sold in the market in Corinth. Yet, Paul is happy to allow Christians to buy and eat that meat. What matters is not whether the *origin* of the food is idolatrous, but whether the food *now* to be eaten is part of a religious rite.

Anglo–Saxon Christians simply have no experience or teaching as to how central food eaten as part of sacred meal is to almost all faiths. One can add that food enjoyed in company of others seems to sustain life and offers a profound experience. Conceptually, food and worship are connected because all seem to offer life and joy. Therefore, food offered to idols seems to be life-enhancing, but is susceptible to demonic exploitation.[86]

In our churches, even the Lord's Supper is usually celebrated outside the context of a proper meal. Perhaps if we celebrated the Lord's Supper in the context of a proper meal (1 Corinthians 11:17–34) then we would understand far better the importance of sacred meals. Sacred meals function to bind communities together and bring worshippers into the sphere of influence of spiritual beings.

---

5. You are invited by a Hindu family to dinner. Do you go?

Yes, you go. Paul says that in eating meals with pagans there is no need to have any doubts (1 Corinthians 10:27). Therefore, eating with those of other faiths does not constitute a pagan act of worship. We are to love all peoples, pray for them, and use any opportunity to evangelize.

---

6. You go to dinner at your Hindu neighbours'. You enjoy a splendid curry. After dinner, they offer you some delicious Indian sweets, but as you are about to take one, your host explains that these sweets have been dedicated in the temple. Do you eat?

While there is nothing inherently "spiritually dangerous" about the sweets, the fact that it has been pointed out by your host implies that, in his mind, the sweets have a special spiritual character.

---

[86] Thus, conceptually, food sex and worship are connected because all seem to offer life and joy. Note here the link between food, sex, and idolatry in Revelation 2:14f.; 20; see also the discussion in S. C. Barton, "Food Rules, Sex Rules and The Prohibition of Idolatry: What's the Connection?" in *Idolatry: False Worship in the Bible, Early Judaism and Christianity* (ed. S.C. Barton; London: T & T Clark, 2007): 141-162. For a contemporary appropriation of the notion of idolatry into the areas of love, money, and power, see T. Keller, *Counterfeit Gods* (London: Hodder & Stoughton, 2009).

Therefore, you thank your host for his kindness but you do not eat. You do not eat, not for your own sake but for the sake of your pagan host (1 Corinthians 10:28–29a). Why? Because if he sees you eating he may believe that you believe that his religion has spiritual merit and your gospel witness is blunted. We may complain that if we give thanks to God why we should be prevented from eating (1 Corinthians 10:29b–30). Paul's answer is that our eating must be shaped by a concern for God's glory (1 Corinthians 10:31) and a seeking after not our own good but the good of the salvation of others (1 Corinthians 10:33). We put the salvation of others before our own pleasures and "freedom."[87]

In my experience, food consecrated in a Zoroastrian fire-temple has been present at ordinary family meals. At these meals, sometimes it is pointed out to me that particular fruits have been consecrated because family members automatically assume that I would not eat them. I do not eat these fruits. If I ate these fruits the assumption of family members would be that I did not see Christ and Christianity as exclusive and unique. Thus, eating does have spiritual significance in the eyes of those of other faiths. Christians must think through the theological and practical implications of food in multi-faith society.

For those Christians converted from other faiths it mean that we must be encouraged seek to love our families and witness to them, rather than cut ourselves off from them because of the anger and rejection directed at us from our families for our commitment to Christ. We must honour our parents, be involved in all social activities (outside of worship), and always be ready to give an answer for the hope that is within us.

---

[87] The issues in 1 Corinthians 8-10 are about idolatry and food offered to idols, and are not the same as the issues about Christians keeping the Torah and the OT food laws in Romans 14-15. While some things are similar (the assertion of "freedom and the principle of concern for the "weak" other), the issue of idolatry in 1 Corinthians 8-10 and the terminology of "knowers" (not the "strong") make the passage different from Romans 14-15. We must not use Romans 14-15 to interpret 1 Corinthians 8-10 since to do so is to miss what is distinctive in 1 Corinthians 8-10.

Further, those converted from other faiths will need the love and practical support of their new Christian family. Many will have come from backgrounds where they found their identity in their family/community/culture. When they come to Christ, they will want to find their identity, friendships, and love in the church. They may find the individualism of many Anglo-Saxon evangelicals and church culture difficult to understand.

Pastors should make a special effort to be hospitable to those Christians from other faith backgrounds. I felt lonely when I came to Christ because I felt rejected by my family. I had lost my family and culture, but did not feel understood or well supported by the church. Women in church must care especially for married women who come to Christ from other faiths. These women may experience hostility and persecution from their husbands and their families. They may be put under strong pressure to participate in family weddings and funerals in the temple. Here the love and support of a godly and mature Christian woman will be critical.

Paul's ultimate pastoral advice in all these matters is to imitate him as he imitates Christ (1 Corinthians 11:1). Let us love others. Let us listen to the OT (1 Corinthians 10:1–13), steer clear of participation in the ultimately demonic nature of idolatry (1 Corinthians 10:18–22), put no barriers in the way of the salvation of others (1 Corinthians 8:7–9:27), and do all to the glory of the true God in Christ (1 Corinthians 8:6; 10:31).

3.4.   Conclusion

The worship of other faiths may be well intentioned but is both empty and, ultimately, evil. The worship of the true God is exclusive. This is of great theological importance for the debate on world religions and inclusivism.

Crucially, it means that the inclusivist position is fundamentally mistaken because world religions inclusivists have not wrestled with sufficient seriousness with the demonic character of other faiths. Demons "co-opt" the worship of other faiths, and hence other faiths are "included" within the sphere of influence of evil powers.

The issue of the interaction of Christians with the worship of other faiths is a matter of great pastoral importance today. The key pastoral principle is: *In love, we must point out that it is seriously wrong for any Christian is be involved as a participant in any act that is intended as an act of worship by the member of another faith.*

4.   Conclusion

For the worship of idols that may not be named,
Is the beginning and cause and end of every evil.

Wisdom 14:27

But 'tis strange;
And oftentimes to win us to our harm
The instruments of darkness tell us truths,
Win us with honest trifles, to betray us
In deepest consequence.

Shakespeare, *Macbeth*

The question of the relationship between demons and idols in 1 Corinthians 10:18–22 is a question of critical importance exegetically, theologically, and pastorally. Paul writes chapters 8–10 as a reply to the concerns about food offered to idols. Paul is attempting to dissuade the Corinthians from attending idol feasts. He points out that the worship of the One God is exclusive and that demons are associated with idols.

In chapter 1, we saw that idols and demons are two distinct entities. Paul defines an idol to be to the pagan god itself as well as its cult image. Idolatry is participation in any act that involves the honour, or invocation, or worship of an idol. Demons are real personal supernatural evil beings. We may classify the demons under the rubric of the principalities and powers, the angels of the nations, and the spirits of the dead giants.

In chapter 2, we saw that the worship of other faiths is both "empty" (it is idolatrous) and, ultimately, "evil." Demons are related to idols because they use their power to enslave humans into idolatry, deceive people into worshipping idols, and "co-opt" the worship intended for idols.

In chapter 3, we considered the theological and pastoral

implication for ministry. Theologically, the ultimately demonic nature of the worship of other faiths strongly supports the doctrine of the uniqueness of Christ and the exclusive nature of the Christian faith for salvation. Importantly, demons "include" those of other faiths within their sphere of influence, and this reality undermines world religions inclusivism.

Pastorally, this is an issue of enormous significance, first, for those who come to Christ from other religions. They must reject all participation in the worship of their former faith, and yet seek to be involved with their family. This will call for spiritual wisdom on their part and the support of the church family.

Evil powers and empty idolatry remains a temptation, a danger, a threat, and a grievous sin for the church. There can never be any compromise with idolatry and any participation in the worship of other faiths.

We live in a multi-faith society. Many in our congregations will want preaching and teaching on their relationships with those of other faiths, not least, on whether they should eat food offered to idols. A church that dabbles in idolatry will arouse the jealous anger of her Lord and the salvation of those professing church members who participate in that idolatry will be at risk if there is no repentance.

There is enormous pressure on evangelicals to conform to the values our pluralistic society, but we must be faithful. Idolatry is no minor sin, but is the sin of sins; it marks the boundary between Christian and non-Christian, between the saved and the damned. The key practical principle is that *any act, which is intended by someone of another faith as religiously significant, is idolatrous and therefore is off-bounds.* While idolatry is always a temptation for Christians (1 Corinthians 10:13) there can be no participation by a Christian in an act intentioned by a pagan to constitute worship.

The church's ministers must urgently preach and teach 1 Corinthians 8–10 and its implications so that Christians reject all inter-faith worship as an involvement in idolatry and the demonic. This is a salvation issue. On this question lies the ultimate fate of millions of souls. Satan and his minions are on the prowl ensnaring the worshippers of other faiths. We need the whole armour of God. My prayer is that evangelical ministers will see the enormous theological and pastoral implications of 1 Corinthians 10:18–22 and teach the truth about other faiths, refute error, rebuke sinful behaviour, and guide in the paths of righteousness.

Let John Calvin have the final word:

> For when men become so futile in their thinking that they offer worship to creatures rather than to God alone, they are ripe for the punishment of being servants of Satan. For they do not find any intermediary position between God and Satan, for which they are on the look-out, but, as soon as they turn their back on the true God, Satan immediately sets himself before them as an object of worship.[88]

---

[88] Calvin, *1 Corinthians*, 219.

BIBLIOGRAPHY

Primary Sources

Aland, B., K. Aland, J. Karavidopoulos, C.M. Martini, & B.M. Metzger, eds. *Novum Testamentum Graece post Eberhard et Erwin Nestle.* 27ᵗʰ ed., corrected. Stuttgart: Deutsche Bibelgesellschaft, 2001.

Bray, G.L. ed. *1–2 Corinthians.* Ancient Christian Commentary on Scripture, New Testament VII. Downers Grove: IVP, 1999.

Mignes, J.-P. ed. *Patrologiae cursus completus: Series Graeca.* 162 vols. Paris: Petit-Montrouge, 1857–1886.

Neusner, J. *The Mishnah: A New Translation.* New Haven/London: Yale University Press, 1988.

Pietersma, A., & B. G. Wright, eds. *A New English Translation of the Septuagint and the Other Greek Translations Traditionally Included under that Title.* New York/Oxford: Oxford University Press, 2007.

Rahlfs, A. ed., R. Hanhart rev. *Septuaginta.* Rev. ed. Stuttgart: Deutsche Bibelgesellschaft, 2006.

Roberts A., & J. Donaldson, gen. eds. *The Ante–Nicene Fathers: Translations of the Writings of the Fathers Down to A. D. 325.* 10 vols. Repr., Grand Rapids: Eerdmans, 1990.

Secondary Sources

Allo, E.-B. *Saint Paul: Première Épître aux Corinthiens.* 2nd Edition. Paris: Gabalda, 1956.

Alexander, P.S. "The Demonology of the Dead Sea Scrolls." Pages 331–353 in *The Dead Sea Scrolls after Fifty Years: A Comprehensive Assessment.* Vol 2. Edited by P.W. Flint & J.C. VanderKam. Leiden: Brill, 1999.

Barton, S.C. "Introduction." Pages 1–6 in *Idolatry: False Worship in the Bible, Early Judaism and Christianity.* Edited by S.C. Barton. London: T & T Clark, 2007.

Barton, S.C. "Food Rules, Sex Rules and the Prohibition of Idolatry: What's the Connection?" Pages 141–162 in *Idolatry: False Worship in the Bible, Early Judaism and Christianity.* Edited by S.C. Barton. London: T & T Clark, 2007.

Bauckham, R.J. "Biblical Theology and the Problems of Monotheism." Pages 187–232 in *Out of Egypt: Biblical Theology and Biblical Interpretation.* Scripture & Hermeneutics Series. Vol 5. Edited by C. Bartholomew, M. Healy, K. Möller, & R. Parry. Milton Keynes/Grand Rapids: Paternoster/Zondervan, 2004.

Beale, G.K. *The Book of Revelation.* NIGTC. Grand Rapids/Carlisle: Eerdmans/Paternoster, 1999.

Beale, G.K. *We Become What We Worship: A Biblical Theology of Idolatry.* Downers Grove/Nottingham: IVP/Apollos, 2008.

Bolt, P.G. "Jesus, the Daimons, and the Dead." Pages 75–102 in *The Unseen World: Christian Reflections on Angels, Demons, and the Heavenly Realm.* Edited by A.N.S. Lane. Carlisle: Paternoster, 1996.

Bolt, P.G. "Towards a Biblical Theology of the Defeat of the Evil Powers." Pages 35–81 in *Christ's Victory over Evil: Biblical Theology and Pastoral Ministry.* Edited by P.G. Bolt. Nottingham: Apollos, 2009.

Calvin, J. *1 Corinthians: Calvin's New Testament Commentaries.* Paperback edition. Translated by J.W. Fraser. Edited by D.W. Torrance & T.F. Torrance. Grand Rapids/Carlisle: Eerdmans/Paternoster, 1996.

Cheung, A.T. *Idol Food in Corinth: Jewish Background and Pauline Legacy.* JSNTSupp 176. Sheffield: Sheffield Academic Press, 1999.

Dawes, G.W. "The Danger of Idolatry: First Corinthians 8:7–13." *CBQ* 58 (1996): 82–98.

Elliott, N. "The Anti–Imperial Message of the Cross." Pages 167–183 in *Paul and Empire: Religion and Power in Roman Imperial Society.* Edited by R.A. Horsley. Harrisburg: Trinity, 1997.

Fee, G.D. *The First Epistle to the Corinthians.* NICNT. Grand Rapids: Eerdmans, 1987.

Forbes, C. "Paul's Principalities and Powers: Demythologizing Apocalyptic?" *JSNT* 82 (2001): 61–88.

Forbes, C. "Paul's Demonology and/or Cosmology? Principalities, Powers, and Elements of the World in their Hellenistic Context." *JSNT* 85 (2002): 51–77.

Gäckle, V. *Die Starken und die Schwachen in Korinth und in Rom: zu Herkunft und Funktion der Antithese in 1 Kor 8,1–11,1 und in Röm 14,1–15,13.* WUNT 2.200. Tübingen: Mohr Siebeck, 2004.

Gardner, P.D. *The Gifts of God and the Authentication of a Christian: An Exegetical Study of 1 Corinthians 8–11:1.* Lanham: University Press of America, 1994.

Goldingay, J.E. *Daniel.* WBC 30. Nashville: Thomas Nelson, 1989.

Halbertal M., & A. Margalit. *Idolatry.* Translated by N. Goldblum. Cambridge/London: Harvard University Press, 1992.

Hays, R.B. *Echoes of Scripture in the Letters of Paul.* New Haven/London: Yale University Press, 1989.

Heibert, P.G. "The Flaw of the Excluded Middle." *Missiology: An International Review* 10.1 (1982): 35–47.

Héring, J. *La Première Épître de Saint Paul aux Corinthiens.* CNT 1.7. Neuchâtel/Paris: Delachaux & Niestlé, 1949.

Hodge, C. *The First Epistle to the Corinthians.* 1857. Repr., London: Banner of Truth, 1964.

Hoehner, H.W. *Ephesians: An Exegetical Commentary.* Grand Rapids: Baker, 2002.

Horsley, R.A. "Consciousness and Freedom among the Corinthians: 1 Corinthians 8–10." *CBQ* 40 (1978): 574–589.

Keeler, T. *Counterfeit Gods: When The Empty Promises of Love, Money and Power Let You Down*. London: Hodder & Stoughton, 2009.

Kistemaker, S.J. *Exposition of the First Epistle to the Corinthians*. New Testament Commentary. Grand Rapids: Baker, 1993.

Lampe, P. "Die dämonologischen Implikationen von 1 Korinther 8 und 10 vor dem Hintergrund paganer Zeugnisse." Pages 584–599 in *Die Dämonen: Die Dämonologie der israelitisch–jüdischen und frühchristlichen Literatur im Kontext ihrer Umwelt/ Demons: The Demonology of Israelite–Jewish and Early Christian Literature in Context of their Environment*. Edited by A. Lange, H. Lichtenberger & K.F.D. Römheld. Tübingen: Mohr Siebeck, 2003.

Lewis, C.S. *The Last Battle*. The Chronicles of Narnia. London: Collins, 1980.

Liddell, H.G. & R. Scott, Revised H.J. Jones. *A Greek–English Lexicon with a Revised Supplement*. (LSJ). Oxford: Clarendon, 1996.

Mody, R.K. "'The Case of the Missing Thousand': Paul's Use of the Old Testament in 1 Corinthians 10:8 – A New Proposal." *Churchman* 121.1 (2007): 61–80.

Mody, R.K. "The Relationship between Powers of Evil and Idols in 1 Corinthians 8:4–5 and 10:18–22 in the Context of the Pauline Corpus and Early Judaism." Ph.D Thesis., University of Aberdeen, 2008.

Morgan, C.W. "Inclusivisms and Exclusivism." Pages 17–39 in *Faith Comes by Hearing: A Response to Inclusivism*. Edited by C.W. Morgan & R.A. Peterson. Downers Grove/Nottingham: IVP/Apollos, 2008.

Newton, D. *Deity and Diet: The Dilemma of Sacrificial Food at Corinth*. JSNTS 169. Sheffield: Sheffield Academic Press, 1998.

O'Brien, P.T. "Principalities and Powers: Opponents of the Church." Pages 110–150 in *Biblical Interpretation and the Church: Text and Context*. Edited by D.A. Carson. Exeter: Paternoster, 1984.

Ortlund, R.C. *Whoredom: God's Unfaithful Wife in Biblical Theology*. NSBT 2. Leicester: Apollos, 1996.

Ovey, M. J. "Idolatry and Spiritual Parody: Counterfeit Faiths," *Cambridge Papers* 11.1 (2002): 1–4.

Pinnock, C.H. "An Inclusivist View." Pages 93–123 in *Four Views on Salvation in a Pluralistic World*. Counterpoints Series. Edited by D.L. Okholm & T.R. Phillips. Grand Rapids: Zondervan, 1996.

Rosner, B.S. *Greed as Idolatry: The Origin and Meaning of a Pauline Metaphor*. Grand Rapids: Eerdmans, 2007.

Schnabel, E.J. "Other Religions: Saving or Secular?" Pages 98–122 in *Faith Comes by Hearing: A Response to Inclusivism*. Edited by C.W. Morgan & R.A. Peterson. Downers Grove/Nottingham: IVP/Apollos, 2008.

Schrage, W. *Der Erste Brief an die Korinther: (1 Kor.6,12 – 11,16.)*. EKKNT 7/2. Neukirchen–Vluyn: Neukirchener, 1995.

Senft, C. *La Première Épître de Saint Paul aux Corinthiens*. CNT 2.7. Neuchâtel/Paris: Delachaux & Niestlé, 1979.

Somerville, R. *La Première Épître de Paul aux Corinthiens.* Vol. 2. Vaux–au–Seine : Editions de la Faculté de la Théologie Evangélique, 2005.

Stackhouse, J.G., ed. *No Other Gods before Me?: Evangelicals and the Challenge of World Religions.* Grand Rapids: Baker, 2001.

Stevens, D.E. "Daniel 10 and the Notion of Territorial Spirits." *BSac* 157 (2000): 410–431.

Stuckenbruck, L.T. "Why Should Women Cover Their Heads Because of the Angels? (1 Corinthians 11:10)." *Stone Campbell Journal* 4 (2001): 205–234.

Stuckenbruck, L.T. "Giant Mythology and Demonology." Pages 318–338 in *Die Dämonen: Die Dämonologie der israelitisch–jüdischen und frühchristlichen Literatur im Kontext ihrer Umwelt/Demons: The Demonology of Israelite–Jewish and Early Christian Literature in Context of their Environment.* Edited by A. Lange, H. Lichtenberger & K.F.D. Römheld. Tübingen: Mohr Siebeck, 2003.

Thiselton, A.C. *The First Epistle to the Corinthians: A Commentary on the Greek Text.* NIGTC. Grand Rapids/Carlisle: Eerdmans/Paternoster, 2000.

Webb, W.J. *Returning Home: New Covenant and Second Exodus as the Context for 2 Corinthians 6.14–7.1.* JSNTSupp 85. Sheffield: JSOT, 1993.

Williams, G.J. "An Apocalyptic and Magical Interpretation of Paul's 'Beast Fight' in Ephesus (1 Corinthians 15:32." *JTS* 37.1 (2006): 42–56.

Willis, W.L. *Idol Meat in Corinth: The Pauline Argument in 1 Corinthians 8 and 10.* SBL 68. Missoula: Scholars Press, 1985.

Wink, W. *Naming the Powers: The Language of Power in the New Testament.* Vol. 1 of *The Powers.* Philadelphia: Fortress, 1984.

Witherington III, B. "Not so Idle Thoughts about *Eidolothuton.*" *TynBul* 44 (1993): 237–252.

Witherington III, B. *Conflict and Community in Corinth: A Socio–Rhetorical Commentary on 1 and 2 Corinthians.* Grand Rapids/Carlisle: Eerdmans/Paternoster, 1995.

Wright, A.T. *The Origin of Evil Spirits.* WUNT 2.198. Tübingen: Mohr Siebeck, 2005.

Wright, N.T. "One God, One Lord, One People: Incarnational Christology for a Church in a Pagan Environment." *ExAud* 7 (1991): 45–56.

Latimer Publications

Latimer Publications

Lightning Source UK Ltd.
Milton Keynes UK
UKOW052307191211

184076UK00001B/17/P